KIDS WHO RULE

The Remarkable Lives of Five Child Monarchs

Charis Cotter

annick press
toronto + new york + vancouver

©2007 Charis Cotter (text)
Edited by Barbara Pulling
Design: Sheryl Shapiro
Maps: Emily Redelmeier

Annick Press Ltd.

We acknowledge the support of the Canada Council for the Arts, the Ontario Arts Council, and the Government of Canada through the Book Publishing Industry Development Program (BPIDP) for our publishing activities.

Cataloging in Publication

Cotter, Charis
　　　　Kids who rule : the remarkable lives of five child monarchs / by Charis Cotter.

Includes bibliographical references and index.
ISBN-13: 978-1-55451-062-7 (bound).
ISBN-10: 1-55451-062-7 (bound)
ISBN-13: 978-1-55451-061-0 (pbk.)
ISBN-10: 1-55451-061-9 (pbk.)

　　　　1. Child kings and rulers—Biography—Juvenile literature.　2. Child queens—Biography—Juvenile literature.　I. Title.

D107.C85 2007　　　　　j920.0068′21　　　　　C2006-905538-6

Distributed in Canada by:
Firefly Books Ltd.
66 Leek Crescent
Richmond Hill, ON
L4B 1H1

Published in the U.S.A. by:
Annick Press (U.S.) Ltd.
Distributed in the U.S.A. by:
Firefly Books (U.S.) Inc.
P.O. Box 1338
Ellicott Station
Buffalo, NY 14205

Printed in China.

Visit us at: www.annickpress.com

Contents

For Zoe, the kid who rules at my house

—C.C.

Introduction

What would it be like to be a king or a queen, to live in a palace, to rule a country—while you were still a kid? How would it feel to sit on a throne and wear a crown? What if your mother, your teachers, and your sisters and brothers all had to bow down every time they came into your presence? And what if you were very, very rich, and had a host of servants to do your bidding?

It might not be quite as much fun as it sounds. This book tells the true stories of five children who became rulers when they were very young. The oldest is a nine-year-old Egyptian pharaoh, born over 3,000 years ago. The most recent is a two-year-old boy chosen to be the Dalai Lama of Tibet, an isolated country high in the mountains of Central Asia. Another is a little girl who became queen of Scotland when she was only six days old.

For these young monarchs, being a king or queen was not all crowns and glory and bossing people around. A regent or advisor ran the country while the children were growing up, and made sure that they learned everything they needed to know to be good rulers. As well as lessons every day in reading, writing, history, and languages, the kids had to learn about government, religion, and diplomacy (which means talking very politely to foreign dignitaries so that you get what you want from them). These young rulers had to grow up fast and take on responsibilities other kids don't have to worry about, like signing treaties, talking to army generals, taking part in very long ceremonies, and giving speeches.

From the beginning of history, kings and queens have stood apart from ordinary people. Many cultures believe their monarchs rule by a divine right that is given to them by the gods. Some kings are considered almost gods themselves. Kings and queens have a duty to protect and guide their people: their lives don't completely belong to themselves.

None of the rulers in this book had an ordinary childhood. Queen Christina of Sweden was made to sleep for a year under the heart of her dead father, which hung in a box above her bed. Then she was brought up like a boy because her father wanted her to be a king, not a queen: she walked, talked, swore, and dressed like a boy until she was in her teens.

Mary Queen of Scots was a queen on the run for the first five years of her life, while the King of England, Henry VIII, did his best to kidnap her. Then she went to live in the French court and saw her mother only once in the next 12 years. Mary had to watch what she ate: a servant once tried to poison her dessert.

King Tutankhamun of Egypt changed his name before he was nine and married his sister. He learned how to shoot arrows while driving a chariot, which required extremely good hand-eye coordination. He also had to watch his back: his guardian, Ay, wanted to be king himself.

Henry Puyi of China had perhaps the most bizarre childhood, living without his parents in the middle of a Forbidden City, cut off from the rest of the world. Servants followed him around with tea, jackets, and a chamber pot. When he was hungry, a banquet was spread before him, but he wasn't allowed to eat it.

The Dalai Lama was chosen to be king and spiritual leader of Tibet by monks following their dreams and visions of the country's next ruler. He too lived without his parents in a huge palace, where he made friends with mice and played games with his servants. He had to take on his role as ruler early, when he was only 15, because his country needed his leadership after it was invaded by the Communist Chinese.

There have been many children who became kings or queens before they grew up. All too often war, disease, and sometimes even murder claimed the lives of their parents. Because females often couldn't inherit the throne, history records many more boy kings than girl queens.

The two girls in this book, Queen Mary and Queen Christina, lived within 100 years of each other, at a time in Europe when women were just starting to occupy positions of authority.

The child rulers in this book were chosen because their stories are so fascinating. They all led extraordinary lives, struggling to find their place in a world where they had surprisingly little power. They are separated by time and place: Northern Europe in the seventeenth century was very different from China in the twentieth. But they were all faced with the same challenge: to grow up fast and lead their people. Never given a choice, they were all destined to become kids who rule.

THE IMMORTAL PHARAOH

Tutankhamun of Egypt

ca. 1341 BCE to 1323 BCE

THE BOY STEADIED HIMSELF AGAINST THE SIDE OF THE chariot as it lurched to one side. It must have run over an uneven patch of ground. The horses adjusted to the slight imbalance and returned to their steady gallop forward. The reins were tied tightly around the boy's waist to free his arms for his bow and arrow. His eyes were fixed on the white tail feathers of the ostrich that was trying to outrun them. His hunting dogs were tearing along behind the bird, nipping at its heels and slowing it down.

The horses knew their job. They had to keep pace with the ostrich at first, then slowly gain on it until the boy was within shooting range.

It wasn't easy, trying to shoot a moving target while bumping along the ground in a small wooden cart harnessed to two horses. But Tut had been training for months, and now he was sure he was ready. Today he was going to bring that ostrich down.

Horemheb too thought the boy was ready. After checking the reins around Tut's waist, Horemheb had given him a quick pat on the shoulder and a nod of encouragement. Horemheb wasn't one to jump up and down and make a lot of noise. He oversaw Tut's training with military precision and a quiet sense of order. A word or a swift glance was all he needed to command obedience from everyone around him. Horemheb was the commander of the Egyptian army, and teaching the pharaoh to hunt and shoot was just one of his many responsibilities.

Tut thought that Horemheb was probably the best soldier in the whole world, and he wanted to please him. Tut worked hard at everything he did. He was only 12, but he was strong and quick to learn. He loved riding bareback across the desert, and he loved the thrill of the hunt. He had been pharaoh for three years, and his life had changed drastically during that time. Just last year he had moved from Amarna, where he had lived all his life, to the palace at Memphis. It was every bit as beautiful as his old home, with its shady courtyards and tinkling fountains. His best friend and sister, Ankhesenamun, had come too, so he wasn't lonely. They could still play Senet, their favorite game, for hours, while they ate figs and sweet cakes and drank fruit wine. But the best part of the move was the time Tut now spent in the Valley of the Gazelles learning to hunt and shoot and ride.

He wanted to make Horemheb proud of him. He wanted that ostrich.

The chariot lurched again, and Tut swayed briefly, then straightened. They were gaining on the ostrich, which was getting

tired after its mad race across the desert plain. The bird veered off to the left, and Tut and the horses and the dogs reacted at the same time, with the boy pulling a bit on the reins with his hip and the horses and dogs turning towards the ostrich. All the hunters seemed to be moving and thinking as one now, intent on their prey, and the horses picked up speed.

A decorated wooden chest found in his tomb shows King Tut in his chariot shooting at his Nubian enemies. Servants follow with fans made from ostrich feathers.

As the chariot pulled almost level with the ostrich, Tut fixed his eye on his target and let loose the arrow. The ostrich screamed and fell. The dogs pounced on it, tearing at its throat.

Tut reined in the horses and circled back to the bird, which lay dying. He dismounted from the chariot and stood panting, sweat pouring down his face.

Horemheb rode up on horseback. He too dismounted and regarded the fallen bird. Then he looked up and into the young king's eyes.

"Well done," he said quietly. "Your timing was perfect this time."

Tut grinned, wiping the sweat from his forehead with the back of his hand.

Horemheb continued his praise. "Those are fine feathers, your majesty. They would make a beautiful fan. I'll get Osret to make one for you. Then you'll always remember the first time you made a solo kill."

Tut laughed, and a great feeling of joy rushed through him. He wanted to start yelling and running in circles, but he knew that wasn't dignified behavior for a pharaoh on the brink of manhood, so he just laughed again.

"Let's hunt again tomorrow," he said.

More than 3,000 years later, an archeologist named Howard Carter stood inside a cramped underground chamber, staring at an ostrich-feather fan that lay on the ground beside a wooden shrine. The brown and white feathers were nearly rotted away. A moon-shaped palm holder covered with gold was embossed with pictures. On one side a young king pursued an ostrich in a chariot, with the reins wrapped tightly around his waist. His bow was taut, ready to shoot. On the other side, the king drove

11

the chariot himself, his servants following with two dead birds. Engraved on the handle was the information that the pharaoh, Tutankhamun, had killed the ostriches that provided the feathers for the fan.

For all that time, while armies and civilizations rose and fell throughout the world, Tut's tomb lay hidden beneath the sand in the Valley of the Kings in Egypt, not far from the banks of the Nile River. Ancient Egyptians believed that dead people could come to life in a world beyond this one. To live in the afterlife, they would need their bodies again, as well as food, clothes, toys, furniture, and treasure. So all these things were buried with Tutankhamun. Although there were some historical references to the young pharaoh, not much was known about him until Howard Carter discovered his tomb in November 1922.

Carter nearly hadn't found King Tut's tomb. He was on the point of giving up his five-year search when he finally got a break. His financial backer, the English aristocrat Lord Carnarvon, had warned Carter he was going to cut off his money, but Carter begged him for one more try, and Carnarvon relented.

Carter knew this was his last chance. He decided to look near the tomb of another pharaoh, Rameses VI, who died about 200 years after Tutankhamun's reign. Ruins of ancient huts stood near the tomb's entrance, built for the workers who dug Rameses' tomb. Carter ordered the huts removed, and one of his workers discovered a set of stairs leading down into the ground.

Carter knew immediately he had found a tomb. His workers carefully uncovered the stairs, which led to a sealed door with Tutankhamun's name written on it in hieroglyphics. That door led into a long passageway that ended with another sealed door. Carter made a hole in the second door and, holding up a small candle, looked in at a room that was full of golden treasures.

THE MUMMY'S CURSE

Sometimes curses were put on Egyptian tombs, especially in the time of the Old Kingdom, about 1,000 years before Tut's reign. They never did much good, though: grave robbers were more afraid of the live tomb guards than of ancient curses. The tale of King Tut's curse was made up by a group of journalists who were tired of hanging around the excavation waiting for news. Even though it wasn't true, it was such a great story that it kept growing until everyone believed it.

The way the story went, there was a curse on Tut's tomb that condemned anyone who entered it. The misfortune started with the untimely death of Lord Carnarvon, Howard Carter's patron, who succumbed to an infected mosquito bite in Cairo six months after entering Tut's tomb. Strangely, at the very moment Carnarvon died, all the lights in Cairo went out, and thousands of miles away in England his faithful dog howled and dropped dead. Carnarvon's brother died suddenly soon after. An Egyptologist working in Tut's tomb died as well. Then a man died from a bad cold after visiting the tomb, and another visitor fell while in the tomb and later died. All of these deaths were blamed on the curse.

The truth was that no curses were found in any inscriptions in Tut's tomb. Many people entered and worked there for years *without* dropping dead, including archeologist Howard Carter. But the press loved the idea of the curse, and so did Hollywood. Countless horror movies feature an ancient curse and an enraged mummy coming back to life.

Statues, thrones, beds, and figures of animals were all jumbled together. The tomb had been robbed, but something must have scared the robbers, because they had run away, dropping a trail of treasure behind them. It was probably the tomb's guards who had piled the disturbed objects in a heap and resealed the doors.

More than 5,000 objects were crowded into three small treasure rooms: baskets, food, wine, clothes, furniture, weapons, and chariots. In the burial chamber lay the greatest treasure of all: Tut's mummy enclosed in a solid gold coffin, which was itself set inside two outer coffins within a stone sarcophagus and topped with four gilded wooden shrines, all perfectly sized to fit together smoothly like a set of Russian dolls. Painted on the surrounding walls were images of Tutankhamun on his trip through the Underworld, aided in his journey by various gods. Because the tomb had been cut into dry rock and sealed tight, the vividly colored pictures looked almost as fresh as the day they were painted.

It took Howard Carter and his colleagues 10 years to record all the objects in Tutankhamun's tomb. Each was photographed and numbered before it was moved. The treasures so carefully preserved there continue to provide us with a rich source of information about ancient Egypt. But they have also revealed pieces of a fascinating story about a boy king who, for a short time, ruled one of the greatest civilizations in the world.

Tutankhamun was born into the royal family of Egypt during the reign of Akhenaten, about 1341 BCE. It's not clear exactly who his father and his mother were. Most of the evidence points to Akhenaten as Tut's father, but the pharaoh may have been Tut's older brother. Tut probably spent his early childhood living in the king's palace in a city called Amarna, with Akhenaten and his queen, the famous beauty Nefertiti, and their six daughters.

The palace at Amarna, built around courtyards with lush gardens and cooling fountains, would have been a lovely place to grow up. Like all the houses in Egypt, it had walls made of mud brick. Small windows set high were hung with matting to keep the sun out. The walls of the palace were brightly painted with scenes from nature, and the floors were covered with rugs or straw mats.

Tut's clothes were kept in baskets or chests, and he slept in a bed, probably covered with a linen sheet. White linen was a popular material for clothes for both men and women, because it was so cool, and Egypt is a very hot country. Lots of clothes were buried with Tut, so we know exactly how he used to dress.

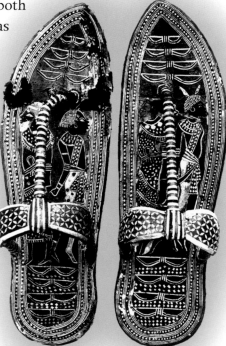

When he was very little, Tut would have gone naked. Once he was old enough to wear clothes, he would have worn a little skirt, with a loincloth underneath. A loincloth was what boys wore for underwear, and Tut was fully prepared in that department for the afterlife—145 loincloths were buried with him! Tut

Every time King Tut wore these sandals he was walking on pictures of his enemies.

also wore tunics and shirts richly embroidered with beads and colored threads. He even had special socks that had a place for his big toe, to wear with sandals on cold desert nights. His sandals had a unique feature: the soles were painted with the images of his enemies, so that every time he took a step he was symbolically crushing his foes.

The food buried with Tut tells us what his favorite dishes were. He was well set up for a few months of good eating, with a nice balance of healthy foods; protein was provided by beef, goat, duck, goose, and fish as well as almonds, chickpeas, and lentils. There were 116 fruit baskets filled with tropical fruit, including figs, dates, and raisins. Tut had fruit juice, fruit wine, and beer to drink, and honey, sweet cakes, bread, and spices like coriander, black cumin, and fenugreek. He was provided with a full set of bronze and copper dishes.

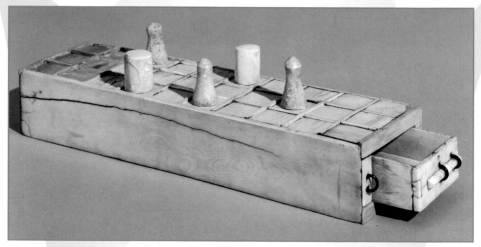

This ivory Senet game is 3,000 years old.

Like any other little boy in Egypt at the time, Tut would have enjoyed rough-and-tumble games like arm-wrestling and a form of leapfrog. There was also a game played with balls where the players knocked down pins, a lot like bowling. Egyptians young and old loved board games, and four versions of the most popular one, Senet, were found in Tut's tomb.

THE OLDEST BOARD GAME

Senet is about 5,000 years old, and may well be the oldest board game in the world. The name means "passing" in Ancient Egyptian, and that's the goal of the game: get your pawns past your opponent's pawns and off the board. The board is divided into 30 squares and the last 5 squares provide the most challenge. As in Snakes and Ladders, these inscribed squares can lead to victory or disaster: One square is "good," one is "bad" (sometimes it's a deadly water trap), and the final three squares are a countdown to the finish "3," "2" and "1." Players use sticks or knucklebones (much as we use dice) to determine how many squares they can move.

Although many games of Senet have been found in Egyptian tombs, and there are several paintings of people and gods playing the popular game, no one has yet found a rule book. Archeologists have spent hours and hours trying to figure out how the game was played. Some think that the game of backgammon grew out of Senet.

But Senet wasn't just a game for Egyptians: it seems to have had a deeper meaning. It was like the game of life: win and you go to heaven; lose and you perish in hell. Senet was certainly considered a lucky game to have with you in your journey to the afterlife—perhaps that's why Tut had four versions of it buried with him in his tomb. Or maybe it was just his favorite game.

Akhenaten died when Tut was about five, and a mysterious figure called Smenkhkare became pharaoh. We know very little about this person, but it is believed that he (or she) ruled for only about four years, before disappearing from the historical record. Tut was crowned pharaoh when he was nine. He was too young to rule Egypt, so two very able officials, Ay and Horemheb, took charge as regents. Ay, the grand vizier, was an older man who had been a powerful figure in Akhenaten's government. Horemheb, general of the armies, was young, strong, and invincible in battle. Between them they managed the country in Tutankhamun's name. It is likely that Horemheb was in charge of Tutankhamun's military training.

The pharaoh was expected to lead his armies in battle, so he had to be a skilled warrior. The traditional training ground for the pharaohs was near Giza, where the pyramids stood. The Valley of the Gazelles provided a rich variety of wildlife for hunting: gazelles, ostriches, lions, and antelopes.

At some point in his childhood Tut married his sister. In ancient Egypt, girls usually got married at about the age of 14 and started having babies right away. Ankhesenamun was one of the six daughters of Queen Nefertiti and Akhenaten, so she was probably Tut's half-sister, and they would have been brought up together. It was considered quite normal, even desirable, for a pharaoh to marry his sister, although ordinary Egyptians wouldn't have dreamt of it. The royal family were almost divine; they held an exalted position somewhere between humans and gods. The gods married their sisters: it made them stronger. So pharaohs did the same, to show their closeness to the gods and to keep their power and wealth in the family.

Tutankhamun and Ankhesenamun lived in a palace in the city of Memphis, near the pyramids at Giza, and they traveled up

A gold engraving on the back of a throne shows
Ankhesenamun tenderly anointing King Tut with oil.

the Nile River to the holy city of Thebes for religious festivals. In Tut's tomb there are many images of him with his wife, all showing great affection between them. In one, Tut sits back in his throne while Ankhesenamun reaches out to put scented oil on his arm. In another, he pours perfume into her hands, and in yet another she gives him flowers. They seem young and happy together, enjoying the pleasures of life.

But a shadow is cast over this image of their marriage by something else found in the tomb: two tiny coffins with the mummies of stillborn babies. Historians believe these were the young couple's children. Tutankhamun died without producing an heir to his throne.

When Tutankhamun was born, his country was 2,000 years old; the pyramids were 1,000 years old; and Egypt ruled as a superpower in the ancient world. Over the course of their history, Egyptians had developed a sophisticated religion based on the

A DANGEROUS WORLD

To us today it seems that Tutankhamun died young, at age 19. But in ancient Egypt, life expectancy was much shorter than it is now. Children were especially vulnerable to attacks by poisonous snakes, scorpions, crocodiles, hippos, and other wild animals. And without our modern knowledge of medicine and cleanliness, many children were killed by stomach diseases and other infections. Parents were so concerned about their children that they made charms and wrote out spells to hang around their children's necks to protect them.

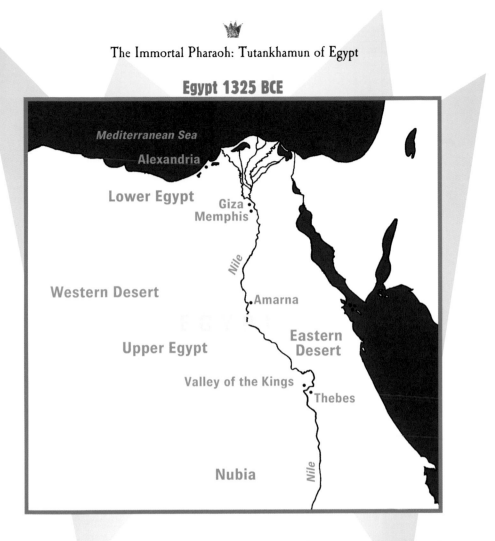

Egypt 1325 BCE

Mediterranean Sea

Alexandria

Lower Egypt

Giza
Memphis

Nile

Western Desert

Amarna

Eastern Desert

Upper Egypt

Valley of the Kings

Thebes

Nubia

Nile

powerful forces of nature. With deserts on the east and west, and the Mediterranean Sea to the north, the country was naturally well protected from invaders, and its civilization had time to grow without outside interference. Fed by plentiful crops grown in the rich Nile Valley, the people prospered.

Traditionally, the power of the pharaoh was central to Egyptian society and religion. The pharaoh's job was to protect Egypt and its people. He had to have a strong army to defend the country, and he also had to keep the gods happy by building temples and carrying out sacred rituals. People believed that as long as the pharaoh fulfilled his duties, the gods would bless their country with good harvests, prosperity, and victory over its enemies. Priests became very powerful, maintaining temples all through the country. Every aspect of life was governed by a different god, and people prayed and made offerings to them.

Akhenaten changed all this during his reign as pharaoh. He claimed there was only one god, Aten, the sun disk, and he banned all other gods. Akhenaten decreed that all the power from the sun went to the pharaoh and his family, so the people had to worship the pharaoh himself. Since only the pharaoh could talk directly to Aten, the priests lost their jobs and many temples closed. People who relied on the temples for their work now had no money. Akhenaten decided to build a new city for this new god, moving the religious capital of Egypt from Thebes to Amarna.

KIDS AT WORK

Like other rich children, Tut was well educated and learned to read and write. But most children living in Egypt at the time did not have the opportunity to go to school. They started working at about the age of five, looking after their younger brothers and sisters, fetching water, and cleaning the house. When they were a little older, they would help in the fields, scaring birds away from the crops, gathering animal droppings to use as fuel, and carrying food to grownups. Girls learned to cook and to bake the many sweet cakes and cookies Egyptians loved. They also learned how to weave beautiful baskets from grasses. The baskets were used for holding food and storing clothes.

Sixty-four pharaohs, including King Tut, were buried in the Valley of the Kings.

After Tutankhamun was crowned pharaoh, the grand vizier, Ay, restored the old Egyptian religion. Temples were reopened or rebuilt, and priests returned to their prominent position in society. Thebes once more became the religious capital of the country and Amarna was left empty to crumble into the sand, only 20 years after it had been built.

When Tutankhamun was about 19, almost old enough to start ruling his country himself, he died mysteriously. He had no heir, so Ay took over and became the next pharaoh. From the moment Tut's body was discovered by Howard Carter in 1922, people began asking questions. Was his death accidental or was he murdered? Did he have a disease that slowly killed him or was he suddenly struck down by a fatal illness?

Modern scientists looked to Tut's mummy for answers, but it had been badly damaged by Carter and his workers when first removed from its coffin. It was hard to tell which injuries were 3,000 years old and which were recent.

23

There were certainly reasons to believe Tut had been murdered. Ay had been running the country with Horemheb for years, and perhaps he felt Tut's coming of age would cramp his style. It wouldn't be the first time a king was helped out of this world by an ambitious regent.

In 2005 some of the mysteries around Tut's death were cleared up, thanks to the technology of the CT scan, a set of X-rays that produce an exact picture of the inside of a body. With the permission of Egyptian authorities, Tut's mummy was carefully scanned. The images showed that his head had likely been injured by the embalmers who removed his brain during the mummification process. But a thigh injury seemed to be an original wound, and probably the cause of Tut's death. His leg was badly broken, with the kneecap detached. Scientists speculated that he had an accident in which he had broken his leg, and that infection had set in and killed him. Otherwise Tut showed all the signs of being a healthy, well-fed young man. There was no indication that he was murdered.

As soon as a pharaoh came to the throne in Egypt, he ordered workers to start building his tomb. It took years to create a suitably magnificent resting place. When Tut died, his tomb was nowhere near ready. They had to use a smaller one intended for someone else.

There must have been a frantic scramble to prepare for Tut's burial. His priests and servants had 70 days after his death— that's how long it took to mummify the body at a special building called the Beautiful House. The first step was to remove the brain; it was pulled out through the nose with a special hook. Next, the kidney, liver, stomach, and intestines were removed through a slit in the torso; they were dried, then placed inside special miniature coffins. Once Tutankhamun's spirit re-entered

This beautiful image of the boy king, carved from wood,
shows his head rising out of a lotus flower, the symbol of rebirth.

his body, he would need all his organs back, so they had to be well protected by the gods until then.

Following this process, the body was laid out for 40 days on a bed of natron, a kind of salt that absorbed moisture. Once the body was completely dried out, it was treated with preservatives made of resins, gums, and oils, then wrapped in hundreds of meters of white linen bandages. Tut's fingers and toes were

THE AFTERLIFE AND THE BOOK OF THE DEAD

The Egyptians worshiped the sun god, Amun-Re, as the symbol of rebirth. Every day the sun traveled across the sky and then died in the west, only to be born again at dawn the next morning when it rose triumphantly in the east. They believed the sun god traveled through the Underworld (the land of the dead) during the hours of the night. Amun-Re vanquished death and darkness when he rose up again in the sky in the morning.

The Egyptians believed that when a person died, his or her life force, called ka, left the body. If that body could be preserved after death, the ka could re-enter the body and bring the person back to life in the magical world beyond this one, known as the afterlife.

Pharaohs and other members of royalty were mummified and buried, and many rituals were performed to ensure their rebirth. A collection of spells, incantations, and prayers was inscribed on papyrus scrolls and placed inside the coffin, serving as a guide to help the deceased navigate the obstacles in the Underworld. This collection of writings has come to be known as *The Book of the Dead*.

fitted with gold caps. Magical amulets and jewelry were placed among the bandages, then the whole mummy was coated with resin to preserve it. A beautiful gold mask was placed over Tut's face, and his mummy was encased in the solid gold coffin.

When it was time for the funeral, the gold coffin would have been placed in a shrine covered with images of cobras for protection. Traditionally, the coffin was put on a wooden sled and draped with flowers. Twelve high officials pulled the sled in a procession from the Beautiful House to the tomb in the Valley of the Kings. Once they reached their destination, prayers and rituals were performed, the most important being the Opening of the Mouth, usually presided over by the pharaoh's heir. Ay performed this rite for Tut. He touched Tut's eyes, mouth, ears and nose in a ceremony that represented the awakening of Tut's senses in his reborn state.

Finally Tut's coffin was taken into the inner burial chamber of his tomb and placed inside two more coffins, a stone sarcophagus. and four gilded shrines. The priests backed out of the burial chamber, sweeping their footsteps away behind them, and sealed the door.

When Howard Carter uncovered the coffin that held Tut's body, he found a faded wreath of flowers, placed there as a tribute to a king who had died too young.

The End of the Story

At the time of Tutankhamun's death, his wife, Ankhesenamun, must have been frightened as well as heartbroken. She wrote a letter to the king of the neighboring Hittites, who had long been at war with Egypt, begging him to send one of his sons to be her new husband. Perhaps she thought she could ward off the ambitious Ay by marrying a strong prince from another country, and thus continue as queen of Egypt.

But the Hittite prince was murdered at the border, probably by Horemheb. There is evidence that Ay himself married the young widow, and then all traces of her disappear. Ay ruled as pharaoh for four years and then died, leaving Horemheb to take over as king. During his 25-year reign as pharaoh, Horemheb tried to destroy all references to Akhenaten, Tut, and Ay. He wanted history to forget them. But although he gave orders for

Tutankhamun's name to be hacked out of monuments and temples, for some reason he left Tut's tomb intact.

The discovery of King Tut's burial site in 1922 captured the imagination of people around the world. Suddenly all things Egyptian were in vogue. Tut had a direct influence on architecture, design, and fashion for years to come. His life has inspired songs, books, and movies. Major exhibitions of his treasures have toured the world's museums. Scientists and historians have put in thousands of hours trying to reconstruct his life and solve the mysteries surrounding his death.

Ancient Egyptians had a saying: "To speak the names of the dead is to make them live again." If this is true, Tutankhamun lives still, as the most famous pharaoh of all.

QUEEN ON THE RUN
Mary Queen of Scots
1542–1587

"MARY, WAKE UP! MARY!"

Mary opened her eyes. It was still dark, but her nurse was shaking her and repeating over and over again: "Mary, you must wake up! God preserve us, God save us, Mary, wake up!"

"What's wrong, Janet?" said the child clearly, sitting up.

"Heaven preserve us," Janet Sinclair murmured, pulling Mary out from under the covers. "You must get dressed as quick as you can, the English are coming, God help us, the murdering devils." She gave a strangled sob.

Mary looked closely at her nurse's face in the flickering candlelight. "Well, then, we must hurry." She pulled off her nightie and was soon dressed in a thick skirt, petticoats, and a warm top. Then Janet bundled her out the door and downstairs.

The hall of Stirling Castle was brilliantly lit with torches, and people were rushing back and forth with bundles and provisions, the women crying, the boys looking scared, and the few men grim-faced.

Mary's mother appeared suddenly, a wool shawl in her arms. "There you are, ma cherie," she murmured as she wrapped the shawl around Mary. "We're off on a midnight adventure, my love." She turned to give some brisk orders to a servant. Tall and stately, she radiated calm among the frantic servants.

Mary waited quietly. She trusted her mother completely, and she knew when to behave. She was nearly five years old, after all, and Queen of Scotland to boot. Her mother turned back to her.

"We have a long trip ahead. Are you my brave girl?"

Mary nodded, but for the first time a flicker of fear ran down her spine. "Where are we going, Maman?"

Her mother gave a shaky laugh. "We're off to the monks at Inchmahome. There's been a battle and the English have won. We must run and hide so they don't find you."

"I see," said Mary. The English were always after her, but her mother managed to keep one step ahead of them. Her mother was very clever and brave, and Mary wanted to be exactly like her when she grew up.

"Off we go," said her mother. Taking Mary by the hand, she led the way out the big doors of the castle. A line of horses stood puffing clouds of warm breath into the cold Scottish night. A footman with strong arms lifted Mary up onto a litter, and her mother tucked some blankets around her. The litter, an enclosed wooden cabin resting on wooden poles, was harnessed to horses ahead and behind. Mary was quite snug and dry inside.

"We'll be there in time for breakfast," said her mother, and kissed her. Then she turned to her horse and mounted swiftly. A servant called out a command and the journey began.

**High on a rocky cliff, Stirling Castle sheltered Mary
from her enemies for the first four years of her life.**

*It seemed an endless night to little Mary, rocking back and
forth as the horses made their way along uneven roads and path-
ways. The air was filled with a damp mist that was not quite rain,
and although Mary snuggled under the blankets, its white tendrils
seemed to lay icy fingers on her.*

*She dozed off again and again, only to be woken by a sudden
lurch of the horses or a shout from one of the other travelers. A few
times her mother rode up alongside and spoke softly to her.*

*Finally, when Mary was so tired she wanted to cry, the horses
drawing the litter pulled up. The mist was even thicker here, a
foggy white blanket that surrounded them. The other horses loomed*

as shadows, the sounds of their harnesses were muffled, and there was a sharp smell of mud and reeds. Mary struggled out from under her covers and looked out the window. Two hooded figures appeared in the mist and spoke to her mother. Then they approached Mary's litter, and the taller one lifted her down.

His hood was scratchy against her skin.

"Greetings, Your Majesty," the monk said in a soft voice. "You'll be coming in our wee boat now across the water to our island. No bloody English will find you there."

He carried her down a steep slope and handed her to another monk, who stood in a small boat. Mary's mother followed, and her nurse, and then the monks pushed the boat off shore. The mists lifted as they left the land behind, and Mary could see water stretching out on all sides to distant hills. She huddled near her mother, cold now.

"We hear it was bad," said the first monk.

"Dreadful," answered her mother. "A massacre. They're saying 10,000 dead, but I can hardly believe it. There was no chance for our poor lads."

"You got away in good time, though?" he asked, pulling on the oars.

"Yes. They'll find no one at Stirling when they get there today," said her mother.

"Look, Your Majesty," said the monk to Mary. "There's Inchmahome. Safe in the middle of the lake. Not even the fairies can find you there."

The island looked impossibly small to Mary, but as they drew nearer, it grew. Finally their boat pulled up to a short pier. Above them rose a little stone church with tall windows.

The second monk lifted the girl in his arms and stepped onto the pier.

"You'll be safe here, never worry," he said to her.

Mary grew up to be a tall, graceful woman with a lovely face and beautiful auburn hair.

It wasn't the first time Mary Queen of Scots had had to run from the English, and it was certainly not the last. Mary Stuart, who became a queen when she was six days old, spent the first five years of her life on the run, barely escaping the clutches of the very scary King Henry VIII of England. Mary was moved from one castle stronghold to another to avoid the English troops, who were intent on capturing her.

TUDOR–STUART FAMILY TREE

Henry VII = Elizabeth of York
(1485–1509)

England – Tudors | **Scotland – Stuarts**

Henry VIII
(1509–1547)

=Catherine   =Anne Boleyn   =Jane Seymour
or Aragon

Mary I   Elizabeth I   Edward VI
(1553–1558) (1558–1603)   (1547-1553)

Henry had 3 more wives
=Anne of Cleves
=Catherine Howard
=Catherine Parr

Margaret=James IV
(1488–1513)

James V=Marie de Guise
(1513–1542)

Mary, Queen of Scots
(1542–1567)

=Frances II France
(1559–1560)

=Lord Darnley

=Earl of Bothwell

James:
VI of Scotland (1566–1625)
I of England (1603–1625)

Only people relevant to Mary are shown
Dates are of reign

When Mary was nine months old, her mother took her to Stirling Castle, high on a rocky cliff by the sea. Here she could keep Mary safe from the English army and, as a last resort, arrange for her to flee to France by ship. Stirling Castle was a huge Scottish fortress with a banquet hall that could seat 300 at a pinch, but during the young queen's stay the guest list stayed much smaller. For Mary Stuart's protection, very few people could get in to see her, and visiting nobles could bring only two servants with them, to avoid anyone trying to take the child by force.

Why did the English want the baby queen so badly? The answer lies in the long and troubled history of three countries: England, Scotland, and France. The English royal family and the Scottish royal family were closely related. Mary's grandmother was King Henry VIII's sister. Mary stood fourth in line to the throne of England, right behind King Henry's three children, Edward, Mary Tudor and Elizabeth.

The Scots and the English were always at war with each other, and Henry figured that if he could marry off his son, Edward, to Mary, he could unite the two countries and rule them both from England. No matter that Edward was only five and Mary just a baby: that's how royal marriages were arranged in those days.

Some very powerful nobles in France had their eyes fixed on Mary as well. Mary's mother, Marie de Guise, came from France, and her brothers, Francis and Charles, were key advisors to the French king. These two schemers wanted to gain control of Scotland and England through their influence on Mary.

So tiny Mary had two countries plotting to use her for their own ends. Although she was already Queen of Scotland, she wasn't officially crowned until she was nine months old. She howled all the way through the ceremony at Stirling Castle, almost as if she knew that being queen wasn't going to be much fun.

When King Henry realized that Marie de Guise was not going to hand over her daughter, he flew into one of his famous tantrums. Vowing to kill as many Scots as he could, he began a campaign of bloody raids against his northern neighbors, burning crops and destroying homes. His campaign was referred to as the "Rough Wooing" of Mary. When a man tries to persuade a woman to marry him, usually by treating her really well, he is said to be "wooing" her. But Henry's intention was to scare everyone in Scotland so much they would agree to the marriage of Mary and his son.

Henry VIII always thought he could get what he wanted by force. He needed a son, but his first wife gave him only a daughter. When the Catholic Church refused to let him divorce her, the king started his own church, the Protestant Church of England, and divorced her anyway. When each of his other wives (there were five more) failed to bear a son, he either divorced them or had them beheaded (except for Edward's mother, who died shortly after giving birth). Henry VIII had finally got his son, and now he was after Scotland.

THE KING WHO WAS A LOUSY FORTUNE TELLER

Mary Stuart was born into a country in turmoil. Her father, James V, had just lost a spectacular battle with the English, and he was so depressed he just gave up and died. (Or so the story goes—he also had a terrible stomach flu.) James V lived long enough to hear that his new child was a girl, instead of the much-needed male heir, and he made a sorrowful prediction about his family's future before he breathed his last: "The devil go with it! It came with a lass, it will gang (go) with a lass." The house of Stewart had begun their rule of Scotland with a woman, Marjory Stewart, and James figured this new queen would be the last Stewart to take the throne.

James V wasn't much of a fortune teller. Mary Stuart's son, James VI, would become king of Scotland and England, and the house of Stuart (the spelling changed when Mary moved to France) went on to rule England for 100 years.

DYING FOR RELIGION

During Mary's lifetime, the tension between Catholics and Protestants grew ugly. Extremists on both sides believed that they were the true Christians and that those who disagreed with them were the agents of the devil. Both Protestants and Catholics were killed for their beliefs.

Until the early 1500s, all of Europe had been Roman Catholic. Many people became dissatisfied with the Catholic Church, which was rich and powerful. The Protestants wanted to do away with the Catholic pomp and ceremony, and to worship God more simply, without all the fancy trimmings. They were called Protestants because they were protesting against what they saw as a corrupt and evil church.

Mary Stuart's family was Catholic, as was the French royal family. But there were many Protestants in Scotland, and their numbers were growing. The Scottish monarch would have to do a very tricky balancing act between Protestants and Catholics.

The Scots never liked to be forced to do anything, especially by the English. They dug in their heels and fought back. But even after King Henry died, and his son, Edward, became king, the English kept up their ruthless campaign. Fighting grew worse, and it ended with a horrible battle at Pinkie Cleugh in 1547, in which 10,000 Scots were killed. When the news of the battle reached her mother, Mary Stuart was taken secretly in the middle of the night to Inchmahome.

The monks hid her in the monastery for three weeks. When the English kept advancing, Mary was moved to another stronghold, called Dumbarton, guarded by French soldiers this time. She lived there for five months, until a treaty was signed between Scotland and France that promised to marry her to the Dauphin Francis, heir to the French throne. The idea was that when Francis became king of France, he and Mary would rule both countries.

By July 1548, it had become too dangerous for Mary to stay in Scotland. Mary was put on a ship bound for France, which meant saying goodbye to her mother. Marie de Guise had to remain in Scotland to help govern the country until Mary came of age. She had kept her daughter safe from the English, but the cost was a very painful parting with her child.

When Mary stood on deck and watched Scotland disappear into the mist, she was only five and a half years old, yet she already had the dignity and composure of someone much older. From the beginning, her mother had taught her to behave like a queen. Mary was tall for her age, quick and intelligent, and she could talk quite comfortably with grownups.

It took 18 rough and rocky days to make the voyage from Scotland to France. Everyone except Mary got violently seasick. She walked out on the deck every day, breathing in the salty sea air and wondering what life would be like for her in France. She hadn't set out alone: she had her best friends with her, four girls all named Mary who had been her companions for some time. Her nurse, Janet Sinclair, came along too.

The French court gave Mary a royal welcome. Believing that Scotland and England were uncivilized countries inhabited by barbarians, the courtiers were curious about this new little queen.

It was the tradition in France for royal children who were engaged to be married to participate in a special ball. The children had to learn the complicated steps of court dances, dance together in public, and exchange kisses. The grownups thought

Mary, Queen of Scotland, and Francis II, who was to become the King of France, were engaged to be married when Mary was five and Francis was four.

this was terribly cute, but it wasn't so much fun for the kids. Mary learned the dances perfectly and made an excellent impression. But Francis, the future king of France, was only four and not so naturally gifted. He was a small, sickly boy who stuttered and fell over his own feet. Mary helped him through and the two children quickly became the best of friends.

Scotland and France, 1550

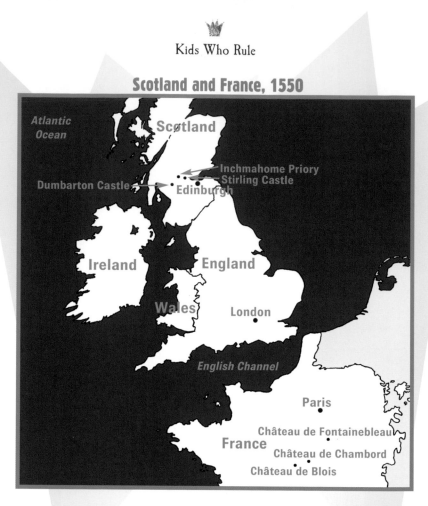

Mary settled into her new life with ease. Although she missed her mother, she was now living in the lap of luxury with the very sophisticated French royals. The French court was large; it included all the nobles, women, and children who were closely connected to the king of France, as well as his servants and chief advisors. The whole entourage moved from place to place, depending on the time of year and how they wanted to amuse themselves. They took everything with them: beds, dishes, clothing, pets, and even wall hangings. A long line of carriages, wagons, horses, and mules carried people and luggage from one grand castle to the next.

When the French court felt like hunting, they went to Château de Chambord in the Loire Valley. Within the 32 kilometers (20 miles) of the castle walls was a vast forest park where they could hunt wild boar, deer, and wolves. They kept their best hunting horses there, and their favorite falcons and hawks. The castle itself was so big that it had more than 300 chimneys. Mary and Francis both enjoyed hunting and became excellent riders.

When the French royalty had business in Paris, the court stayed right downtown at the Palais du Louvre, which is a famous art museum today. That wasn't quite so pleasant as being in the country. Cities really smelled in those days, with garbage piled in the streets and human sewage floating down the gutters. The main Paris market was nearby, too, with all its odors of rotting vegetables and blood from freshly killed animals. It was much more fun to go to the lovely Château de Fontainebleau with its beautiful lake, or to the Château de Blois, where orange and lemon trees grew indoors in a separate wing of the palace called the Orangerie.

When they were in the mood for hunting, the French court stayed at the Château de Chambord, a fairy-tale castle with 300 chimneys and a huge park filled with wild animals.

One of the big advantages of living in France for Mary was the education she received there. All the royal children were educated together, so she and Francis were taught the same subjects by the same tutors. As a result, she learned what a boy would learn: to think for herself.

Surrounded by French-speaking children and adults, Mary quickly became fluent. Most of the other subjects she studied were geared toward preparing her to deal with the politics of

GIRLS AND EDUCATION

In the sixteenth century, the education of women was a hot topic in Europe. Until that time, girls from poorer families learned to sew and cook; the wealthier ones might pick up a smattering of Latin or Greek from their brothers' tutors. But girls in general were considered inferior to boys and not worth educating. Their role in life was to marry and have children.

The Italians changed all this. During the Renaissance, with art, music and literature blossoming, women began to have more influence. They were prized at court for their conversational skills. To be witty and sparkling among gentlemen, women had to be able to talk about more than embroidery and babies' diapers. So little girls began to be educated along with their brothers. This practice gradually spread throughout Europe.

When Mary was 12, she gave a talk in Latin for the French court. Knowing that her sophisticated audience would understand her essay perfectly, she spent weeks preparing. Her topic? The importance of education for women.

ruling a country. She needed Italian and some Spanish to be able to speak to visiting ambassadors and dignitaries. Studying rhetoric, a formal type of speech used in debate, taught Mary how to analyze an opponent's strengths and weaknesses. Classical languages (Latin and Greek) helped her converse and write with wit and grace. History taught Mary the stories of earlier kings and queens, showing her their triumphs as well as their mistakes.

Mary worked hard at her schoolwork, although no one ever accused her of being a brilliant student. She did a good job, but her real talents lay elsewhere. She was a wonderful dancer and loved music and poetry. Like her mother, she could charm anyone, even her enemies. Diplomats would often leave her presence basking in the warm glow of her personality, realizing only later that she had neatly avoided giving them what they wanted.

Mary also had the rare ability to inspire love and loyalty in others. She showed great generosity and concern for her servants all her life. Whenever she had to let any of them go, she made sure they had another job, and she arranged for pensions for the older servants, so that they could live comfortably in their old age.

When Mary was 12 it was decided that she would have her own household. The dauphin moved off to his own establishment, and the royal nursery broke up. Mary now had her own set of servants, and she could host dinner parties and balls. Whenever the court moved from one palace to another, her belongings were packed up and carted along in her own carriages.

There was always some kind of entertainment going on at the royal court. Mary showered gifts and money on her favorite performers: musicians, clowns, jugglers, actors, and dancers. When Mary wasn't hunting, or skating, or learning how to dance ballet, she was going to masquerade balls and royal banquets. Exotic birds were a delicacy featured at these dinners;

people ate birds we wouldn't think of putting on a plate today, such as swans, peacocks, and herons.

Although Mary's life in the French court was luxurious and privileged, she was not free to do whatever she liked. Mary's uncles, Charles de Guise and Francis de Guise, kept an eye on her manners and advised her on everything she did. For all her education, accomplishments, and personal charms, Mary was still a pawn in their chess game to control France and England.

Mary had only one visit from her mother after she moved to France, but they remained close by writing letters back and forth. Marie de Guise guided her daughter as well as she could from a distance. She gave her advice about what do to and say on formal occasions, as well as how to get along with her governess. Parts of their letters were written in a secret code, out of a fear of spies. The French and Scottish courts were hotbeds of schemes and secret plots, and it was difficult to know whom to trust. When Mary was nine, there was a plan to murder her by

PLAYING HOUSE

With servants to help with everything from getting dressed to taking a bath, fashionable ladies and girls in the French court sometimes found very ordinary tasks exotic and fun. They considered it a great treat to pretend to be servants and do some cooking. Mary and her best friends, the four Marys, had their own kitchen built so they could "play house." Their favorite recipe was a kind of marmalade called cotignac. It was made with sugar, powder of violets, and quinces—a fruit something like an apple or a pear. The girls took great delight in boiling up the fruit for hours and then making jam.

poisoning her favorite dessert, frittered (fried) pears. The culprit was one of Mary's own Scottish servants, but luckily the plan was discovered before Mary was hurt.

When Mary was 15 and Dauphin Francis was 14, their relatives and advisors decided it was time for them to marry. On April 24, 1558, the marriage agreement between France and Scotland was sealed during one of the most luxurious spectacles France had ever seen. A procession of soldiers, courtiers, musicians, church officials, and the entire royal family filed through the streets of Paris to Notre Dame Cathedral.

Mary wore a white dress, unusual for a bride in those days, but it dramatically set off her pale white skin and red hair. The dress was thickly embroidered with diamonds and other jewels, and her gold crown was set with sparkling sapphires, emeralds, pearls, rubies, and more diamonds. Gold and silver coins were

In Mary's time, only very wealthy people could afford books, like this illustrated prayer book called the *Book of Hours*. Mary would have been able to read both the Latin and the French shown here.

tossed into the crowd of spectators, nearly causing a riot, while the aristocrats celebrated the wedding with two banquets and a ball. Mary wrote to her mother that she was gloriously happy.

Mary's wedding to Francis marked the end of her childhood. But she would not come into her rule as queen in Scotland until she turned 18. During the next three years, Mary suffered a series of crushing blows that turned her life upside down. Her troubles started in July 1559, when her father-in-law, Henri II, the king of France, died as the result of a jousting injury. (Jousting is a sport in which two knights fight on horseback with long spears called lances.) Francis became king, with Mary

A FAIRY-TALE PRINCESS

Brought up in the sumptuous French court and surrounded by extravagance and splendor, Mary had expensive tastes from a very young age. By the time she was nine she owned a huge collection of dresses made of the most luxurious fabrics, and her jewelry filled three brass chests to the bursting point. She especially liked clothes embroidered with precious jewels.

Because of her status as a queen, Mary dressed quite formally, and had many occasions to show off her lovely clothes and sparkling jewels. When she was 10, she had her portrait painted wearing some of her jewelry: a gold necklace with rubies and diamonds, a string of pearls, earrings, and a jeweled band around her headdress.

Mary loved animals and wherever she went she was always accompanied by her favorite pets. At one point she had 16 dogs (mostly spaniels and small terriers) that traveled with her from palace to palace. She even owned a royal bear!

as his queen, but they were both too inexperienced to rule the country. Francis's mother, Catherine de Medici, and Mary's uncles fought over the control of France like dogs over a bone.

There was a new queen in England by now: Elizabeth I. She was a Protestant, and England became a Protestant country. Although Elizabeth and Mary would never meet, their lives were intricately connected. Mary stood next in line to the English throne, and Elizabeth was worried that Mary and the Catholics would try to take her crown by force.

Elizabeth's fears were fueled by the actions of Mary's conniving uncles. When Francis and Mary became king and queen of France, the uncles took the opportunity to declare that Mary, not Elizabeth, was the true queen of England. Although Mary's uncles were eventually out-maneuvered by the clever Catherine de Medici, and lost their influence in the French court, the results of their scheming haunted Mary for the rest of her life. Elizabeth would never trust Mary, and ultimately this distrust contributed to Mary's downfall.

Just a year after her father-in-law died, Mary lost her mother. Marie de Guise had been embroiled in a civil war in Scotland, with the Protestants and the English lined up against the Catholics and the French. The Protestants won, and Marie succumbed to a fatal illness shortly afterwards. Mary was devastated by her mother's death. Even though they had been separated for many years, she had depended on her mother's wisdom and guidance. Now she was alone.

There was one more blow to come. Six months after her mother's death, her sickly husband, who was always fainting or throwing up, developed a dreadful earache and fell into a fever. Although Mary and Catherine de Medici nursed Francis around the clock, he too died.

Mary went into deep mourning. Overnight she changed from queen of France to persona non grata (the one who isn't wanted) at the French court. Francis's younger brother, Charles, who was only 10, became the new king, and Catherine de Medici took over as regent to rule France until he came of age. Mary suddenly had no standing in France.

Mary could have stayed in France with her relatives. Or she could have accepted one of the offers of marriage that started pouring in from all over Europe. But she had been brought up to be a queen, and a queen she was going to be. In August 1561, at the age of 18, she set sail for Scotland, 13 years after she left its shores as a fugitive. With her sailed her faithful four Marys and 12 ships full of clothes, furniture, servants, and horses. Mary Stuart had grown from a precocious child into a sophisticated woman, and she was ready to take on her role as the reigning monarch of Scotland.

The End of the Story

Assuming the rule of Scotland proved to be tricky for Mary. It was now a Protestant country, and although Mary was allowed to practice her Catholic faith, there were many zealous Protestants who disapproved. The most vocal was John Knox, a fiery Protestant preacher who denounced the queen at every opportunity, saying her dancing was evil and her religion the worship of the devil. Mary did her best to balance the various political factions, and at first she managed pretty well.

It has been said that Mary's downfall was her impulsive nature. Unlike Queen Elizabeth I, who avoided marriage and remained independent, Mary married three times, and her last two husbands were scoundrels—both of them ended up involved in murders that stained Mary's reputation. Her first,

Lord Darnley, arranged to have his friends kill Mary's Italian secretary while Mary stood by, pregnant and helpless to stop them. Her second husband, Lord Bothwell, had Lord Darnley murdered so that he could marry the queen and rule the country at her side. Many people in Scotland believed Mary had been involved in that plot, and civil war broke out between those who supported her and those who didn't. Eventually she was forced to give up the crown of Scotland in favor of her little boy, James, who was just 13 months old.

Mary was once more taken to a castle on an island, but this time she was a prisoner. Lochleven was a small fortress, home to the Douglas family. Two of the sons of the family secretly supported Mary's cause and plotted her rescue. After nearly a year in captivity, Mary managed to escape by dressing as a servant and slipping away by boat while the family was at dinner. Mary fled to England, hoping that Queen Elizabeth I would help her.

Mary had made many efforts to make friends with her royal cousin over the years. She had written letters asking to meet with her, but Elizabeth had always refused. Mary kept hoping that Elizabeth would relent and show her some kindness. But Elizabeth's chief concern was to protect herself: Mary was the next in line to her throne. All the Catholics in England were itching to push the Protestants out of power, which made Mary the perfect leader for them. Elizabeth could not afford to let her go free. Mary stayed imprisoned in various castles in England for 19 years.

Over that time, there were many Catholic-supported plots to rescue Mary and overthrow Elizabeth. There was never strong proof that Mary herself was involved, but the English were suspicious. Finally, when a scheme to kill Elizabeth was uncovered, the English queen reluctantly agreed that Mary was too dangerous to live. She was condemned to death at the age of 44.

Mary Stuart showed great courage as she was led to her execution, and she tried to comfort her weeping servants. She wore a petticoat the color of blood, a dramatic gesture. The executioner bungled the job, and it took three strokes to cut off her head. Her little dog had hidden under her skirt, and he ran out and lay down in her blood, refusing to leave his mistress.

In a twist of fate, Mary won the struggle for power in the end. Sixteen years after her execution, Elizabeth died, and she was succeeded by Mary's son James, King of Scotland. He became James I of England, and for 100 years the Stuarts ruled Scotland and England.

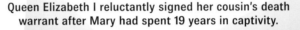

Queen Elizabeth I reluctantly signed her cousin's death warrant after Mary had spent 19 years in captivity.

THE GIRL BORN TO BE KING

Queen Christina of Sweden

1626–1689

CHRISTINA LAY RIGID BETWEEN THE CLAMMY SHEETS in the big bed. The darkness was so deep she couldn't even see her mother lying beside her, but she could hear her crying. Her mother had been crying for months, every day and every night, from the moment that Christina's father had been killed in the war. But the little girl was used to the crying. What made her lie so stiffly, scarcely breathing, sat in a small silver box at the head of the bed: her father's heart, cut from his dead body and wrapped in satin. Christina had nightmares that the heart would slip from its box and land between her and her mother, soaking the bed in blood. Or she would think she heard it beating, the sound growing louder and louder until she woke up, sweating and trembling with fear.

Christina tried to remember her father before he went to war: his crinkly blue eyes, his blonde hair and beard, the way he threw his head back and laughed, the times he'd scooped her up in his arms and carried her about the castle. But all she could think about was that shriveled heart.

Her mother's tired weeping was interrupted by a hiccup. Christina moved her legs restlessly. Why couldn't her mother stop crying? Christina had learned to dry her own tears by digging her nails into her hands. And why did her mother droop around the castle all day dressed in black? There were horses to ride, dogs to play with, a huge forest to explore. Who wanted to stay cooped up in a castle in a long clumsy dress while the boys had all the fun?

I'll never be like her, vowed Christina, moving as far away from her mother as the bed would allow. I'm not going to be a useless woman imprisoned by castle walls. I'm going to do what I like, and I'll be as good as a boy, just like my father said. Thinking of her father reminded her of his heart, wrapped in its satin shroud in the little box just inches away from her head. She gripped her hands in tight fists, and began to count fiercely to herself. It always worked. Sometimes she counted up to 300, sometimes 500, but eventually she would sleep.

Christina was seven years old, and she was queen of Sweden.

At the time when Christina became queen, girls were not considered smart enough or strong enough to rule a country. Boys became kings: girls married them. So kings wanted sons— but it didn't always work out that way. When Christina was born in 1626, her mother, Queen Maria Eleonora, had already had two babies die. Sweden was a country at war. Christina's father, King Gustavus Adolphus, was a brilliant general, and he was often away from the country, leading his troops in battle

Sweden 1630

Norwegian Sea

Kingdom of
Sweden

Stockholm

Stegeborg Castle
Nyköping

Brandenburg

Paris

France

against their many foes. His people loved and admired him. But
before his reign there had been bloody turmoil in Sweden, as the
nobles and the royal family struggled for power. The king knew
that only a strong monarch could hold the country together, and
he wanted a boy as his heir.

A very strange thing happened the night of Christina's birth.
Everyone was hoping for a boy so much that when she arrived
they believed she actually was one. Baby Christina was covered
with hair, and her body was partly hidden by a caul—a thin
piece of skin that usually falls off when a child is born. The

attendants sent word to the king that he had a son. But when they removed the caul and had a good look, they were horrified to realize their mistake.

No one was brave enough to tell the king, who was known for his violent temper. Finally his half-sister, Katarina, picked up the baby and went to her brother's room. She presented him with his daughter, and the king took a long look at the tiny creature. Instead of getting angry, he held the little girl close and smiled down at her. "Since God has given me a girl, I hope she will be worth a son to me," he said.

From that moment on, Christina was destined to be king. Her father decreed that she be brought up like a boy, educated like a boy, and treated as much like a boy as possible. She even dressed like a boy sometimes. She learned to ride horses, shoot, and fight with a sword. Christina's favorite toys were lead soldiers, and her favorite pastime was riding a horse recklessly through the woods, with her beloved dogs running along beside her.

King Gustavus adored his daughter and took her everywhere with him. When he went riding, he put her in front of him on his saddle. The Swedish people smiled when they saw the pair coming, the tall, handsome king and the small girl who sat up very straight, curious about everything she saw. Once, when she was very young, the king brought Christina with him to visit a neighboring castle. The nobleman who lived there wanted to give the king the royal gun salute of 50 cannons, but he was worried that the loud noise would frighten the child. King Gustavus told him to go ahead, saying that Christina must learn to live a soldier's life. The cannons were fired with a tremendous roar. Christina clapped her hands in delight and cried for "more bang! more! more!"

Christina sometimes attended the king's meetings with the important men of the kingdom. She sat quietly by his side, listen-

Before he went away to war, King Gustavus Adolphus presented Christina as his heir to the Riksdag (the Swedish parliament).

ing for hours to the solemn fellows with their long beards, even though she didn't understand much of what they said. As long as she was with her father, Christina was content.

When she was with her mother, she wasn't so happy. Queen Maria Eleonora seemed not to like her daughter very much. Maybe it was because Christina had been so odd-looking as a baby, with her hairy little body and her bright blue eyes. Or maybe the queen was jealous because her beloved husband was so devoted to the child. Maria Eleonora was a rather strange woman in any case, and the longer she lived, the stranger she got. She went to extremes in everything. She showed signs of delicate nerves, and she was subject to lengthy crying fits. Some of her behavior was understandable; Maria Eleonora hated Sweden and was permanently homesick. When the king first met

Christina lived in Tre Kroner Castle, a huge medieval fortress surrounded by a moat. It was big enough to house hundreds of people as well as the Riksdag.

her, she was a beautiful princess in the Brandenburg court, far away across the sea. She was accustomed to court life there, where the weather was milder, the stoves warmer, and her companions more refined and well educated. Art, music, and literature were part of her daily life. Life at Tre Kroner Castle in Stockholm was very different.

Sweden in the 1620s was a remote, cold northern country. The roads were bad, farming was primitive, and most of the people lived in rough log houses. In the depths of a Swedish winter, daylight lasted only four brief hours, and for the remaining twenty the country was plunged in darkness. The Swedes had their own culture, rich in history, myth and legend, but it all seemed very odd and rustic to the young lady from Brandenburg. The queen made it clear to everyone who met her that she despised her new country and its inhabitants. She never learned the language properly, and she surrounded herself with her own "court"—companions, servants, and clowns she had brought with her from Brandenburg. The clowns were a collection of undersized people who were all physically unusual—dwarfs with huge heads and hunched backs. She dressed them as jesters, in brightly colored jackets strung with bells that tinkled when they walked. This kind of amusement was the fashion in Brandenburg, but it seemed bizarre to the Swedes. Christina was frightened of these peculiar little people, with their grownup faces and their small, twisted bodies.

To make matters worse, a couple of mysterious incidents occurred while Christina was a baby, and it was whispered that her mother was trying to kill her. Once, a huge ceiling beam fell down and just missed Christina's crib. Another time, a maid dropped her on the floor; Christina hurt her shoulder, and it was crooked for the rest of her life. Most likely these were just accidents, but the queen was so disliked that rumors spread.

One cold day in November, Christina's father came to her room and lifted her in his strong arms. He carried her into a big hall, where all the men with the long beards were gathered. This was the Riksdag, the Swedish parliament. The king sat on his throne and began to talk, with Christina huddled by his side. Christina, who was not quite four, couldn't understand all the words, but she knew something important was happening, because her dear father was very sad. Gradually she began to understand that her father was going away to war, and her mother was going with him.

A few days later, when it came time to say goodbye, her father hugged her tightly and kissed her. He started to put her down, but Christina tugged on his beard to prevent him. She had rehearsed a farewell speech with her nurse, and she whispered it fervently into his ear. The tall, mighty king broke down and began to cry, and Christina did too. She didn't stop for three days. This worried her nurse, because Christina was not the sort of child who cried easily. Now, however, it seemed as though her heart would break.

In those days it took ages to travel anywhere. When people went away, they were gone for months, even years. Even a letter

DON'T DRINK THE WATER!

When Christina was growing up, she wasn't allowed to drink water. Sewage systems in seventeenth-century Sweden were primitive, and most water was contaminated with dangerous bacteria. Everyone drank beer or wine instead.

Christina hated both. But she was always thirsty, so she cooked up a plan. She noticed her mother kept a bottle of rosewater—water perfumed with rose petals—in her closet. Queen Maria Eleonora used the rosewater to wash her face, and it was a great luxury. Christina started sneaking into her mother's room after dinner and taking a drink. When Queen Maria Eleonora caught her in the act, she gave Christina a beating. So Christina stopped drinking altogether. She became dehydrated and developed an ulcer on her breast and a dangerous fever.

As a compromise, her mother decided she would allow Christina to drink "small beer," a weak form of beer that poor people drank. It had less alcohol but apparently an extremely nasty taste. The Queen of Sweden would probably have given anything for one cool, fresh glass of clean water.

took weeks to arrive. Sweden was a great distance from the battle-fields of Europe, and Christina heard no news of her parents for a long time.

For the next two years, Christina lived with her Aunt Katarina and her family in Stegeborg Castle, south of Stockholm. Despite missing the king and queen, Christina was happy there. She had six cousins to play with, and her aunt was a warm, mothering person who was fond of her little niece. But on her sixth birthday, the dreadful news came. The king had been killed in battle. Her beloved father would never be coming home again. Christina's world would never be the same without her champion—he had loved her so much, and made her feel so safe and happy. Now she was filled with inconsolable grief.

Before he left for the war, King Gustavus had had a premonition that he might die in battle. Because Christina was so young, the king had arranged that, if he did not return, the country would be run by a group of five regents, led by his faithful best friend and advisor, Baron Oxenstierna, the grand chancellor of Sweden. He also appointed three special tutors to teach Christina everything she would need to know to become a wise ruler. Baron Oxenstierna would guide her until she came of age.

Christina did not automatically become queen when her father died. The Swedish people also had a say in the matter. The Swedish parliament represented all the citizens of the country. There were four groups, or estates, in the Riksdag: nobles, the clergy, burghers (people who lived in towns), and peasants (farmers). The Riksdag met to pass laws and to approve or oppose the king's actions.

After King Gustavus died, the Riksdag had to approve the choice of Christina as queen. The first three estates agreed, but the peasants weren't so sure. They wanted to see her. Once more,

An engraving of Christina's father, King Gustavus Adolphus II,
on his deathbed. Christina's mother mourned him for years
and kept his heart in a little box near her bed.

Christina faced a hall full of solemn men with long beards. This time she didn't have the comfort of her father at her side. She sat on a throne placed on a golden carpet, and 90 footmen dressed in livery (fancy outfits that all matched) lined up on each side of the room. The 500 members of the Riksdag knelt down before her.

Even though she was only six, Christina knew how important it was to make a good impression on these men. She sat up straight and kept alert and quiet throughout the long, boring ceremonies. But although the members of the Riksdag certainly noted her good behavior, it was her resemblance to her much-loved father that won the day. King Gustavus had been a hero to his people. Christina had inherited not only his blonde hair, blue eyes, and high forehead, but also his sense of dignity and composure. The peasants were convinced, and the Riksdag accepted her as their queen.

Queen Maria Eleonora, filled with grief, slowly made her way back to Sweden with the body of her husband. When she arrived in Stockholm, she decided she must have Christina with her all the time, because the little girl looked so much like her father. So she took Christina away from her cousins in Stegeborg, and they went to live at the queen's private castle at Nyköping.

Then began the nightmare years. Maria Eleonora clung to the child and would barely let Christina out of her sight, even for her lessons. All of the castle's rooms were draped in heavy black velvet; the king's body wasn't buried until 19 months after his death, and every day the queen would throw herself upon his coffin and weep. Eventually, a grand state funeral took place, and Christina and her mother moved back to Tre Kroner Castle in Stockholm. But Queen Maria Eleonora kept the king's heart in a gold casket at the head of her bed, and she made Christina sleep with her. The little girl grew very thin and pale.

Baron Oxenstierna had been overseas all this time, dealing with state matters and the ongoing war. When Christina was 10, Oxenstierna came back to Sweden, and he put his foot down hard. He sent the queen away to live in a lonely castle, and he brought Christina's Aunt Katarina and her family to Stockholm to live with the young girl again. The queen raised a fuss, but there was nothing she could do. Christina was now under the protection of the grand chancellor, and he was determined to carry out her father's wishes to make her a king, or as close to a king as a girl could be.

Christina's unorthodox education, so carefully planned by her father, was unheard of for a girl in Sweden at the time, and exceeded the expectations for boys as well. A key element was physical activity: in those days girls didn't usually get much exercise. Christina's father made sure that Christina would have

Girls' clothes may have been elegant and beautiful, but they were heavy
and required tight corsets. Here Christina is shown in Tre Kroner Castle
with Stockholm harbor in the background.

the same opportunity a boy would have to become strong and physically fearless.

Baron Oxenstierna himself coached Christina in the art of government and politics. A tutor named Gustaf Horn taught her the languages she would need to read widely and communicate with important visitors from abroad. Christina had grown up speaking German with her parents, French with her cousins, and Swedish with her servants. Now she learned Latin, Ancient Greek, Spanish, and Italian as well. Johannes Matthiae, a Lutheran clergyman, taught her history and religion. In Christina's time, religion played an enormous role in everyday life. Civil wars were fought within countries between Protestants and Catholics, and people were killed for their religious beliefs. Sweden was a Protestant nation, and it was vital that the Swedish monarch be a Protestant too. Christina loved Matthiae, calling him "papa," but she hated sitting through hours of long, dull sermons. What she really liked to do was tear around outside on a horse with her third tutor, Axel Banér. Christina lived half her life outdoors, and as a result, she grew up to be a crack shot and an excellent rider.

According to the memoirs Christina later wrote, as a girl she got up at four o'clock every morning and worked for 12 hours a day on her studies. She claimed she was a brilliant student who astounded all her teachers with her abilities. While this is probably a bit of an exaggeration, there is no doubt Christina worked very hard, and she certainly was clever. Every afternoon, she and Oxenstierna would meet to discuss government affairs. The baron was a wily old fox who knew all the tricks of governing and diplomacy. But Christina's favorite subject was ancient history. She loved reading about the heroic exploits of Julius Caesar and Alexander the Great. Christina liked the idea of a world filled with danger, where if you were strong and brave you could always win.

Although Christina didn't have much use for women, she admired Elizabeth I of England, who had died just 23 years before

While she was growing up, there was nothing Queen Christina liked better than galloping through the parkland on her favorite horse.

Christina was born. She felt that Elizabeth's strength of purpose was that of a man, not a woman, and Christina too was determined to be as powerful as a man in every way. Bursting with energy and with curiosity about the world, she was extremely strong-willed—a polite way of saying that she was stubborn. To make herself strong, she kept her rooms very cold in winter, and on hot summer days she would ride her horse furiously to work up a sweat. She preferred to eat the plain fare of a working soldier: dried beef, salt herring, and bread and cheese. She wore boy's clothes, kept her hair short, and developed an abrupt, loud way of talking that alarmed her maids.

GIRL? OR BOY?

No doubt about it, Christina had a license to be a tomboy. When she was 10, after her mother was sent away, Christina had a makeover: her hair was cut short like a boy's, the royal tailors made her boy's breeches and shirts, and the royal cobblers made her boy's boots. From that moment on Christina was brought up as a prince, and she reveled in the freedom. But when she was 16, her mother and other members of the court were alarmed at the rude, gangly figure she had become, and there were fears that such a strange creature would never find a husband and produce an heir. Baron Oxenstierna and her tutors had gone too far.

So Christina had another makeover: she grew her hair long and was given a closetful of beautiful dresses to choose from. Two elegant ladies-in-waiting were instructed to teach her how to be more feminine. With the exception of her wild, glorious rides in the royal hunting grounds, she had to wear women's clothes all the time.

Christina didn't seem to mind this transformation too much, although she did grumble a bit. When it came time for her coronation, she played a trick on Oxenstierna and all her advisors: she told them she was going to wear a soldier's uniform for the great occasion, just as her father had done. There was a tremendous flap, with Oxenstierna finally begging her to wear a dress. She kept up her deception till the last minute, when she appeared in a gorgeous silver gown, just as she had always intended.

Thirteen was a momentous age for Christina. Her tutors Axel Banér and Gustaf Horn both died suddenly. And then her dear Aunt Katarina died after a long illness. It was also the year Christina had to appear before a formidable panel of judges from the Riksdag for her examinations. They asked her questions on history, religion, politics, philosophy, and languages. The Riksdag wanted to determine whether she was fit to be queen, testing her knowledge as well as her reactions under pressure.

As it turned out, Christina did brilliantly on her examinations. She answered the questions the learned men put to her intelligently and calmly, and when it was all over the representatives from the Riksdag smiled and told her she was as good as any prince. That comment would have made her father very, very happy.

For the next five years Christina regularly attended meetings of the Riksdag and began to make some state decisions. When she turned 18, the long years of careful planning and schooling were over. In a magnificent ceremony at Tre Kroner Castle, she was crowned Queen of the Swedes, Goths, and Vandals; Great Princess of Finland; Duchess of Estonia and Karelia; and Lady of Ingria. The funny-looking little baby had grown up to rule the great kingdom of Sweden.

The End of the Story

Christina ruled Sweden for only 10 years, from 1644 until 1654. Then she gave up her throne, declared her cousin Charles her successor, and left the country. There were many reasons for her decision, and none of them was simple.

Christina had always been curious, and she liked to learn new things. Once she was queen, she invited famous people, including philosophers and mathematicians, to come to the Swedish

THE DIVINE RIGHT OF KINGS

Like many people of her time, Christina believed in the divine right of kings, which held that a king (or queen) was chosen by God and blessed with greatness. That person would always carry the specialness of being a king within him, whether he actually ruled a country or not. A king had a sacred duty to his country and his people, and the people around him treated him with great respect, and sometimes fear, because his rule had been bestowed by God.

Unless a ruler's sense of duty and responsibility was very strong, it would have been hard for him ever to admit that he had made a mistake, or to let anyone stop him from doing exactly what he wanted. Christina would come to a point in her life when she had to decide between her duty and her desires. Her understanding of the divine right of kings played a key role in her final decision.

court for intellectual discussions. But such visits were never enough. Christina always wanted more: more thundering cannons, more challenging ideas, more exciting experiences, and more fame. She felt left out of things in Sweden, far from the sophisticated courts of central Europe. She was never happy with the Lutheran religion, and she secretly decided to become a Catholic and to leave Sweden.

When a ruling king or queen gives up the throne, the act is called abdication. Abdication is a very serious step; in today's world, Christina's decision would be similar to a person quitting her job, leaving her family, and giving up her religion. In Christina's time, she would also have been seen as turning her back on a duty God had chosen for her. Her decision to become a Catholic made it seem that she had betrayed her country.

Baron Oxenstierna was brokenhearted. During the abdication ceremony at the Riksdag, he refused to take the crown from Queen Christina's head. Her tutor Johannes Matthiae was blamed for her conversion to Catholicism, and he lost his job as bishop of Stängnäs. But no one was to blame for what Christina became: she was her own person. She had her mother's love of sophistication and her father's courage and intellectual curiosity. She believed she was chosen by God to be special, whether she ruled Sweden or lived in a foreign court in Europe.

Christina finally settled in Rome. She continued to act like a queen, bossing people around and holding court in her grand house, and she gained a bad reputation by hosting wild parties and taking lovers. She loved nothing better than a good argument, especially about religion, and she had many happy disagreements with the Pope.

Queen Christina remained a clever, articulate woman who always had something interesting to say. She died in 1689 at the age of 62. She had never let being a woman stop her from what she wanted to do, and she decided that being queen of Sweden wasn't going to stop her either.

THE MAKE-BELIEVE EMPEROR

Emperor Puyi of China

1906–1967

PUYI SNUGGLED CLOSER TO HIS NURSE, AR MO. HE WAS *sleepy and warm.*

"Nearly bedtime," Ar Mo murmured.

"Nooooo," he replied, but he didn't really mean it. Ar Mo's arms were soft, and she smelled sweet, like the white jasmine flowers in the garden. His eyes closed.

Suddenly there was a loud knocking in another part of the house, then running footsteps, then a whole lot of people talking at once.

Puyi sat up and looked at Ar Mo. She was as startled as he was, but she tried to quiet him.

"It's all right. It must be some late visitors," she began. But the racket was getting closer, swelling up outside the room they were in. As the door burst open, a crowd of people rushed in like an angry wave flooding a sandcastle on the beach.

Ar Mo jumped up, still clutching Puyi, who screamed and clung to her neck. Everybody was talking at once: his father, his mother, some servants, and many large men Puyi had never seen before.

His father's face was pale, and he looked strange and sick. "You must go with these men, Puyi," he said. "They have come to take you to the Imperial Palace. The dowager empress is asking for you."

"No!" screamed the terrified boy. Puyi jumped down from his nurse's arms, ducked under his father's legs, and took off out the door. Behind him the noise rose wildly again, with women screaming, men cursing, and somebody yelling, "Catch him!"

Puyi headed straight for the back room, where his hiding place was. He scrambled into the cupboard and shut the door, holding it fast as his heart beat loudly in his ears. But the babbling voices followed close behind, and soon the door was wrenched open.

His father looked down at him sternly.

"Puyi, you must come!" he ordered, grabbing the boy by the arm.

Puyi kicked and screamed and cried as he was dragged out. Soon he was making as much noise as the crowd of grownups. Ar Mo spoke softly with his mother, and people began to leave Puyi's room. Ar Mo sat down and started to rock him.

"You must go, little one," she whispered. "But I will come with you."

Against all royal protocol and tradition, the next emperor of China was accompanied by his wet nurse in the royal palanquin that carried him from his father's house to the Forbidden City. There the dying Dowager Empress Cixi lay waiting for him. The little boy saw an ancient, wrinkled face peeking out at him from behind a curtain. That set him off screaming again.

"Give him some candy," the old lady croaked to her servants. But Puyi didn't want candy. He wanted Ar Mo, who had been

Puyi with his
father and little
brother, Pujie.

Puyi was only two and a half when he was taken away from his
family to live in the Forbidden City as the Emperor of China.

left outside the door. He threw himself on the floor, and kicked
his feet and kept screaming. He was two and a half, after all, and
screaming was what he did best.

From behind the curtain came a raspy laugh. "What a naughty boy," said the old lady with some satisfaction. "Take him away."

Despite Puyi's naughtiness, the dowager empress had made up her mind. She had the power to appoint the new emperor, and she thought the little screaming one would do very well. For more than 50 years she had been the most powerful figure in China, ruling from behind the throne. Young emperors were easy to control, and as soon as they grew up, she found a way to get rid of them. Puyi's father, Prince Chun, was a nervous, indecisive sort of person, and the empress was sure she would have no trouble from him. The doctors said she was on her deathbed, but she didn't really believe them. She had been very sick, it was true, and she had eaten a huge bowl of crabapples and cream that had violently disagreed with her. But she was a tough old lady, and she thought she would get better.

The empress didn't get better, though. She died two days after her midnight meeting with Puyi. The little boy became a permanent resident of the Forbidden City—as the Supreme Emperor of China, the Son of Heaven. For the next 16 years Puyi lived shut inside its high red walls.

About 500 years before Puyi was born, the Emperor Yongle had built the Forbidden City as a royal sanctuary in the heart of Beijing. Designed to be a city within a city, safe from attack and outside influences, it took 14 years and 200,000 workers to complete. The Forbidden City occupied a rectangle about one kilometer (.75 miles) long and .8 kilometers (.5 miles) wide, and it was protected by 10-meter (33-foot) walls and a moat seven meters (20 feet) deep. There were towers at each corner of the rectangle and gates in each wall.

Inside the walls, the city was laid out in an intricate maze of palaces, walled courtyards, temples, bridges, and gardens. Many

Forbidden City 1912

North Gate

A

B

C

West Gate

East Gate

South Gate

Moat

This is a rough sketch of the Forbidden City, showing the location of the buildings mentioned in the story: Punishment Palace (A), Palace of Mental Cultivation (B), and Palace of Cultivation of Happiness (C).

of the roof tiles were yellow, the special color that only the emperor was allowed to use. Everything possible was done to create an exquisitely beautiful hidden city for the emperor, filled with all he could desire. Over the years the Forbidden City became the cultural center of China. Everything new and beautiful found its way there: valuable treasures such as jewels, porcelain, and precious manuscripts, as well as talented musicians, actors, and artists.

The Forbidden City lies in the heart of Beijing, China's capital.
It was the home of Chinese emperors for 500 years.

Twenty-four emperors lived out their lives within the
Forbidden City's high red walls, along with their wives, children,
courtiers, and servants. Although it could be a bustling, lively
place (as many as 10,000 people lived there at one point), it was
also considered a holy site where the emperor could communicate
directly with God. According to Chinese tradition, the emperor
was an exalted figure greater than all other human beings; he
alone had the right to speak to heaven. In the Forbidden City,
the emperor was surrounded by rituals to support his lofty position and keep him at a distance from the world.

By the time Puyi became emperor of China in 1908, the Qing
dynasty (the royal family) was losing its grip on power. China's
government wasn't working, and different groups fought over
who would replace it. Everything was falling apart, and the
royal court no longer ruled the country from within the walls of

the Forbidden City. When Puyi was six, China became a republic, and he was forced to give up his position as supreme leader.

The royal family was still respected in China, however, and life in the imperial court continued much as it had for centuries. Four key women helped to maintain the royal rituals. These were the consorts, wives of former emperors who were now dead. The rulers of China were allowed to have several wives each. Once an emperor died, the most important wife became the dowager empress, and the others became dowager consorts. They stayed in the Forbidden City for the rest of their lives. The four old women still living there when Puyi was a little boy did their best to preserve their privileged way of life.

When Puyi entered the Forbidden City at the age of two, it was as if he had stepped 400 years back in time. The inhabitants lived as if they were in medieval China, preserving all the traditions of the imperial court. It was considered undignified for the emperor to walk, for example, so Puyi was carried everywhere

A palace in the Forbidden City

on a litter or in a special sedan chair. According to an ancient Chinese tradition, all the servants in the Forbidden City were castrated men called eunuchs. Puyi couldn't go anywhere without a procession of eunuchs to cater to his every need. Because most people weren't supposed to look at the emperor or even to see him, one eunuch went ahead making a kind of honking noise. This was to warn everyone that the emperor was coming and they should get out of the way double quick. Then came the two head eunuchs, followed by Puyi on his litter, with two more eunuchs on either side. They were followed by a line of eunuchs carrying everything that might be wanted on the walk: medicine, tea and cakes, a teapot, hot water, umbrellas, extra clothes, and a chamber pot (in case Puyi had to pee). The eunuchs walked silently, showing great respect for their emperor.

At first, when Puyi was feeling frisky and wanted to get down and run, the eunuchs would gather up their long robes and try to run after him. This proved too awkward, so after a while the whole procession would stop and wait while Puyi had a little run, then proceed when he felt like "walking" again.

Anyone meeting Puyi, even his parents, had to kowtow to the emperor: they had to get down on their knees and touch their foreheads to the ground nine times, to show how exalted he was and how humble they were.

The emperor's special shade of yellow was used for all Puyi's personal items. The lining of his clothes was yellow. So were his hats, belts, cushions, sedan chair, dishes—even the reins for his horse. This too emphasized how special the emperor was, and how different from ordinary people. When Puyi's brother Pujie first came to play with him in the Forbidden City, Puyi threw a fit when he saw yellow on the lining of his brother's jacket. Pujie quickly learned not to wear that color again.

FIRE IN HIS HEART

When Puyi first came to the Forbidden City, no one could control him except his nurse, Ar Mo. He had some splendid tantrums, and the eunuchs who were supposed to look after him were often at their wits' end. Their solution? They bundled Puyi into a room not much bigger than a cupboard and locked the door. Then they left him to scream until he tired himself out. While this was going on, the eunuchs would look at each other and say, "The Lord of Ten Thousand Years has fire in his heart. The best solution is for him to sing a while to disperse the flames." Later, Puyi got his revenge. It was the emperor's privilege to have eunuchs beaten whenever he desired, and Puyi regularly lost his temper and ordered this punishment. There was even a special building called the Punishment Palace where these beatings sometimes took place.

It was not uncommon in China for screaming children to be locked away until they recovered their tempers. Puyi's brothers and sisters were disciplined the same way at his father's house. Traditionally, Chinese children were allowed to do pretty much whatever they wanted until they reached the age of about four. Then they were expected to be obedient, quiet, and respectful of their elders. Poorer children had to work alongside their parents, whether cooking and doing housework (girls) or in the fields or shops (boys). Wealthier children were expected to work hard at school, because a good education was highly valued.

THE IMPERIAL DRAGON

In Chinese mythology, the dragon is the lord of water. Oceans, rivers, rain clouds, and mists are all governed by the fierce and powerful creature. For hundreds of years, a five-toed dragon symbolized the Chinese emperor's strength. No one but the emperor could use the five-toed dragon as a decoration.

Throughout the Forbidden City, the imperial dragon adorned carvings on ceilings, walls, gates, and buildings. It was also found on the emperor's clothes, his dishes, and his possessions. The national flag sported an imperial dragon, and his throne was called the Dragon Throne.

The imperial five-toed dragon, shown here on a door in the Forbidden City, was the symbol of the emperor's power and majesty.

Perhaps the strangest traditions in the Forbidden City were the rituals around food. There were no set mealtimes. When Puyi said he was hungry, the word was passed from servant to servant until it reached the building where the food was cooked. Almost immediately, 100 servants in clean uniforms would proceed to the Palace of Mental Cultivation, carrying tables, the imperial dishes, and a huge amount of food. The food was laid out in the emperor's special yellow porcelain dishes that were emblazoned with the imperial five-toed dragon. It was the tradition to serve 25 dishes to Puyi; this number had been reduced from 100. They included duck, poultry, pork, beef, vegetables, and bean curd (tofu). There was even a special dish to honor Puyi's ancestors, called Ancestor Meat Soup. One month, when Puyi was four, the palace records showed that he had eaten 90 kilograms (200 pounds) of meat and 240 ducks and chickens.

Of course nobody could eat that much. All this food was just for show. What Puyi actually ate were the rather plain meals cooked by the dowager consorts' chefs. The fancy buffet was cooked ahead of time and sometimes the same dishes were put out day after day, going rotten and crawling with maggots. But the food had to be presented this way, because it was the tradition.

Another expensive imperial tradition held that the emperor should never wear the same thing twice. Many tailors were kept busy, using up reams of cloth, hundreds of buttons, and many spools of thread to make new silk tunics, waistcoats, and jackets. When Puyi had worn his clothes once, they were discarded.

It was a very strange life for a little boy. At first Ar Mo cared for Puyi. She nursed him with her breast milk, comforted him when he cried, and slept with him in his bed at night. Although Puyi didn't see his real mother again till he was eight, his father, Prince Chun, visited him briefly every couple of months.

Puyi had no one to teach him right from wrong, except Ar Mo. All the other servants treated him like a god. Ar Mo tried to give him a little guidance. She had a calm, peaceful air about her, and Puyi clung to her side. The dowager consorts, who were always scheming to get control of the young emperor, resented Ar Mo's influence on the boy. They had kept Puyi's mother away because they didn't approve of her, and when Puyi was eight they sent Ar Mo away too. They didn't even give Puyi a chance to say goodbye.

Puyi called all of the dowager consorts "mother." They provided him with food from their kitchen, and every day he made an official visit to exchange formal greetings with them. But that was the extent of their communication. When Puyi was sick, all the dowager consorts made visits to his room with their servants, but none of them showed him any affection. Once, when Puyi was quite small, he got indigestion from eating too many chestnuts. Dowager Empress Lung Yu decided the best cure would be to put him on a diet of rice porridge for a month. Puyi was so hungry he ate the stale bread used to feed palace fish. Nobody seem to care or even to notice that the little boy was starving.

After Ar Mo left, Puyi had to make do with eunuchs for company. They dressed him, fed him, played with him, and told him ghost stories about the statues and carvings of animals in the Forbidden City, which supposedly had magical spirits and could come to life. Puyi loved the stories and always begged for more, but he got so scared he couldn't be left in a room by himself.

When Puyi reached his eighth birthday, he began his schooling in earnest. He had already learned to read and write. Now some other little boys were brought into the Forbidden City to be his classmates. One was his younger brother, Pujie; the others were sons of noblemen. The students and teachers treated Puyi with great respect in the classroom, lining up and bowing to him at the beginning of each day. If Puyi was bad and made a fuss or didn't learn his lessons, they beat one of the other kids instead, because no one was allowed to strike the emperor.

The schoolrooms were located in a big, empty building called the Palace of the Cultivation of Happiness. From eight until eleven in the morning, Puyi and his schoolmates studied classical Chinese and Confucian texts. (Confucius was a Chinese philosopher whose values and ideas had formed the basis of Chinese society for hundreds of years.) Puyi also studied Manchu, the language of his ancestors.

He wasn't particularly good at any of his lessons. What Puyi really liked to do was watch the long line of ants in the tree outside the school window, as they carried food to their nests. As he grew older, he loved to read adventure stories about knights and

Surrounded by high red walls, the Forbidden City was once the center of culture and power in China. By the time Puyi came to live there, the streets, courtyards, and elegant palaces were nearly empty.

magic, and he would make up his own stories and illustrate them. But none of his teachers encouraged him in these skills, because they weren't considered important. Neither was math, science, or geography, so Puyi didn't learn much about the outside world. He didn't even know where China was located on a map.

When Puyi was 11, the chaos of China's politics suddenly broke into his secluded life. A powerful army officer, General Zhang Xun, had decided to restore the monarchy, and he had the support of a strong faction of royalists, including Puyi's tutors. For 12 days Puyi was a real emperor again, signing proclamations. Throughout Beijing, people hung out imperial flags emblazoned with dragons and wore court robes, hats with peacock feathers, and false pigtails, to show their loyalty to the emperor. (The pigtail was the traditional hairstyle worn by royalists.)

But the situation could not last. When a republican pilot flew a small plane over the Forbidden City and dropped three bombs, Puyi's attendants hustled him into his bedroom for safety. The bombing didn't do much damage, and only one eunuch was hurt, but it signaled the end of Puyi's brief return to the throne. The republicans took over the country again, people threw away their false pigtails, and the Forbidden City returned to its sleepy routines.

Puyi's life was shaken up two years later with the arrival of a messenger from the outside world. Reginald Johnston, a Scotsman who had spent 20 years in Asia, had been hired to teach Puyi English, but he ended up giving the boy a crash course on life beyond China's borders, with an emphasis on the British Empire. As a result, Puyi developed a mad crush on everything British, from clothes to afternoon tea. Using Johnston as his model, he transformed himself into a proper little English gentleman, complete with waistcoat, tie, and cufflinks. Puyi chose an English name, Henry, after one of his heroes, King Henry VIII. He gave his brother and sister English names too—William and Lily—and began speaking a strange mixture of Chinese and English, which annoyed his Chinese tutors.

Puyi as a young man. He grew up in privileged isolation and in many ways remained a prisoner for most of his life.

Before he met Johnston, Puyi had harbored a deep-seated fear of white people. He found it strange and spooky that, instead of black, their hair and eyes could be any of various colors. The eunuchs didn't help, telling him that white people carried canes to beat people with and that their trousers were pleated because they couldn't bend their legs. When Puyi first met Johnston, with his upright military bearing, gray hair and blue eyes, the boy was terrified. But his fear slowly changed to respect.

Johnston had a passion for royalty and a sincere affection for his pupil, and he became Puyi's loyal friend. He cherished a hope that some day the monarchy would be restored in China and Puyi would rule as a true emperor. In the meantime, despite his love of Chinese culture, he encouraged Puyi to take on the manners and values of an Englishman, including mastering the art of small talk and using a knife and fork instead of chopsticks.

Johnston didn't approve of the Chinese pigtail, so Puyi cut his off, much to the alarm of the dowager consorts and the entire Chinese court. Johnston insisted that Puyi wear glasses because he was half-blind without them. Although the old ladies declared that glasses would make the emperor look weak, Puyi eventually got his specs. Johnston encouraged Puyi to make occasional trips outside the Forbidden City, and he supported Puyi's desire for a telephone. Even though this request was seen as a threat to their influence, the dowager consorts finally gave in. Soon, in a spurt of juvenile glee, Puyi was making crank calls to famous actors and ordering restaurant meals to be sent to false addresses.

Johnston's influence spread to nearly every part of Puyi's life. The boy started reading newspapers voraciously and learning everything he could about politics. He tried to understand how his country worked and to figure out his place in it. When Puyi was 15, he had a power struggle with Dowager Consort

Duankang. He felt it was time to become involved in hiring and firing employees, and he tried to assert himself. Duankang sent for his mother and grandmother, and gave them such a terrible scolding about Puyi's behavior that they begged Puyi to apologize. Puyi reluctantly agreed. But two days later, tragically, his mother killed herself. Some people thought it was because she was so terrified by Duankang and so full of shame about the whole affair.

The dowager consorts grew more and more concerned about Reginald Johnston's influence on Puyi. The boy was showing signs of growing into a man who would want to make his own decisions. If he left the Forbidden City, the dowager consorts would have to leave too, and so lose all their privileges. They decided it was high time that Puyi got married and produced an heir. Once Puyi was married, they reasoned, he would no longer need a tutor.

Puyi wasn't interested in girls. He dreamed of leaving China and studying at Oxford University in England, as Johnston had done. He and his brother Pujie cooked up a plot to escape, but when they asked Johnston for help, the Englishman refused, worried that his involvement might cause problems between Britain and China. Puyi was devastated. He wanted to live life as himself, not as a pretend emperor manipulated by the dowager consorts or the Chinese warlords.

But it was not to be. The consorts gave him four photographs of young women they approved of, and Puyi chose two of them: Wan Rong, a beautiful, educated young woman of 16 as his first wife, and Wen Xiu (who was rather plain and only 13) as his second wife. Both weddings to took place when Puyi was 16, with celebrations that lasted five days. Many expensive gifts were given to the brides and their families, and a glorious

85

wedding procession for the first wife wound through the city of Beijing. But Puyi hadn't wanted to get married, and he showed little interest in either of his wives. Reginald Johnston's

Beautiful Wan Rong, a well-educated girl from a noble family, was 16 when she became Puyi's first wife.

role as his tutor officially ended, but Puyi still depended on him as a trusted advisor.

Two years after his weddings, Puyi's make-believe life as emperor of China came to an abrupt end. Feng Yuxiang, a warlord who disapproved of spending money on Puyi and his court, marched into Beijing and took control of the city. When his troops surrounded the Forbidden City, Puyi was forced to leave and find sanctuary in his father's house. He would never again live within the high red walls of the ancient city.

The End of the Story

Puyi was eager to embrace the world he had been sheltered from for so long. When he reached his father's house after leaving the Forbidden City, he said, "I had no freedom as an emperor. Now I have found my freedom." But, sadly, Puyi was destined to be a puppet all his life. The scenery would change as he moved from place to place, but he was always manipulated and always in some sort of prison.

After he left the Forbidden City, Puyi needed to find a safe haven away from the chaos of Beijing. The Japanese were planning to take control of China, and since they thought Puyi would be useful, they welcomed him into their country with open arms. A few years later they installed him as the emperor of a new state in China they dubbed "Manchukuo."

Puyi's life had taken a cruel turn. He had no real power in his new role, and he was being used by China's enemies to oppress his own people. For the next 16 years he had all the trappings of an emperor: the title, a mansion, a luxurious lifestyle. But the majority of Chinese people considered Puyi a traitor. Wan Rong, his first wife, became addicted to opium and died in prison many years later. Wen Xiu, his second wife, divorced him.

THE UNLUCKY NORTH GATE

In China, south was considered the most fortunate direction, because the south was associated with sun, warmth, and fertility. Invaders and bitterly cold weather came from the north, so it was the least lucky direction. All buildings in the Forbidden City faced south, as did the main entrance, the great South Gate. The North Gate was used as little as possible by the royal family.

However, after the republicans came into power in China, they took over the South Gate for their own use. When Puyi got married, his first wife had to enter the Forbidden City via the North Gate, and this was considered a very bad omen for his marriage. Sure enough, the couple was never happy. You could blame their conflict on the unlucky influence of the North Gate. But picking a wife from a pile of photographs and getting married at age 16 against his will might have had something to do with their unhappiness as well.

When the Japanese were defeated in the Second World War, Puyi was imprisoned for five years in the Union of Soviet Socialist Republics, China's neighbor to the north. Chinese Communists took control of China in 1949, and Puyi was shipped back to his homeland. He expected to be executed, but the Communists had something else in mind. Puyi's extravagant life as emperor had made him public enemy number one. If the Communists now running China could reform him, it would be a triumph for their cause. Puyi was taken to a prison where those who were deemed to be wrong-thinking citizens were subjected to endless lessons on what it meant to be a good Communist.

For the first time in his life, Puyi had to learn to live with other people as an equal. He never was much good at looking after himself—all those years of being carried around the Forbidden City and waited on hand and foot had left their mark. He was always the last to be dressed, he dropped things, he misplaced his belongings, and he could never quite get organized. But he did what his captors wanted of him: he said he regretted his former life and was sorry for all the terrible things he had done. Puyi became a model Communist citizen, eager to humble himself at any opportunity and to obey all the rules of the Chinese Communist Party.

After nine years in prison, Puyi was released. The Communists were pleased with their transformation of the evil emperor into a responsible citizen. One of the first things he did after being released was to take his fellow prisoners on a tour of the Forbidden City, which had been made into a museum. Puyi dutifully showed them the palaces and courtyards where he had lived for so many years in his make-believe kingdom.

Puyi was given a job at the Botanical Gardens in Beijing, and he puttered around doing some light gardening in the mornings. In the afternoons, he worked on his memoirs. With the help of another writer, he eventually completed the story of his life, and it was published and widely read. Puyi married again, this time to a Communist Party member. He died from cancer at the age of 61.

Nearly 30 years after Puyi was cremated, his widow obtained permission to have his ashes buried at a cemetery near the Qing dynasty tombs south of Beijing. Four former emperors were buried there, along with many other members of the royal family. Puyi had joined his ancestors. He would always be remembered not as the strongest, or the wisest, or the most powerful emperor of China, but as the last.

BORN (AGAIN) TO RULE (AGAIN)

The Dalai Lama

1935–

AS SOON AS LHAMO HEARD THE DOG BARKING OUTSIDE, *he jumped up and headed for the door. Barking meant visitors. Nothing was so much fun as visitors. His mother scooped the boy up and kissed him, laughing.*

"Wait and see who it is, little one. They don't all come to see you!"

A group of solemnly dressed merchants stood at the door, accompanied by a servant. While they were bowing and being polite to his mother and father, Lhamo wriggled out of his mother's arms and ran to hide behind the door. He'd be able to watch things from there. Soon the visiting servant trooped off to the kitchen to make tea for everyone, and Lhamo trotted after him.

Lhamo was only two and a half, and everyone was his best friend. He chattered away while the stranger made the tea, and soon he was sitting in the man's lap, playing with the prayer beads around his neck.

"Mine!" Lhamo said insistently, tugging at the beads. "My beads!"

The servant smiled. "You can have them if you tell me who I am."

Lhamo grinned and kept tight hold of the beads.

"I know who you are—Sera Lama! Sera Lama!" answered the boy, laughing again.

The servant sat perfectly still and stared at the little boy.

Lhamo pulled at the beads again. "Now give them to me. They're mine!"

The man took off his beads and gave them to the boy. "Yes, they are yours," he said softly. Then he put Lhamo down on the floor and went to talk to his parents.

The next day the visitors returned. This time they were dressed as monks, not merchants, and the servant turned out to be the head monk.

"His name is Kwetsang Rinpoche," whispered Lhamo's mother. "He wants to ask you some questions."

"Game!" cried Lhamo, jumping up and down. "My friend wants to play with me!"

The other monks were very serious and quiet, but Kwetsang took Lhamo by the hand and smiled at him.

"Just look at these things here on the bed," he said. "Pick out the ones that are yours."

Lhamo walked over to the bed. It was a strange game, really, and with all those grownups staring at him he lost a bit of his bounce. On the bed lay four strands of prayer beads, some small drums, and some walking sticks. He looked at them carefully. Then

he chose some beads and handed them to Kwetsang. He looked at the drums, and picked up the shiniest one. He gave it a couple of taps and then put it back and chose one that looked a bit older. He handed it to Kwetsang. Next he examined the walking sticks, picked the one he liked the best and gave it to Kwetsang.

"Thank you," said the monk quietly. He had a peculiar look on his face, as if he were going to cry or maybe shout. The other monks were staring at him. Lhamo got a little scared and ran to his mother, who picked him up and squeezed him tight.

"Why are you crying, Mummy?" said the boy. "What's wrong?"

On that cold winter day in 1937, in a remote village, the monks had found their fourteenth Dalai Lama, the spiritual leader and king of Tibet. Life changed completely for Lhamo Dhondrub. He was taken away from his parents to a monastery with his six-year-old brother, Lobsang Samten, for company. Lhamo still saw his parents, but he never again lived with them. He had joined the long and sacred tradition of the Dalai Lamas of Tibet.

A series of dreams and omens had led the monks to Lhamo's home, where they conducted tests to see if the boy was the reincarnation of the thirteenth Dalai Lama, who had died four years earlier. *Reincarnation* means "born again." Tibetans believe that when the Dalai Lama dies, he is born again into a new life somewhere in the vast country of Tibet. Lhamo Dhondrub passed the tests with flying colors. Kwetsang Rinpoche was indeed a lama (a holy teacher) from the monastery at Sera—he had disguised himself as a servant, and the child had no way of knowing this. The prayer beads, drum, and walking stick Lhamo chose had all belonged to the thirteenth Dalai Lama. The monks believed that Lhamo recognized both his old friend Kwetsang and his belongings from his former life.

The Dalai Lama at an early age. His life changed completely when he was named the fourteenth Dalai Lama.

Three signs helped the monks find the person they were seeking: a moving corpse, a fungus, and a vision in a lake. The first sign came from the thirteenth Dalai Lama's corpse. His body had been sealed in a salt-lined box with its head facing south, but when monks opened the box they found that the head had turned to face northeast. They put it back facing south, but a few days later it turned northeast again. The second sign was a huge fungus, something like a giant mushroom, in the shape of a star that grew up overnight on the east side of the thirteenth Dalai Lama's tomb. The monks interpreted both the first and the second signs to mean that the new leader would be found in northeastern Tibet.

The third sign came in the form of a vision to Reting Rinpoche, the regent of Tibet, who would rule the country until the new Dalai Lama was old enough to do so. The regent spent many days praying and then went to the sacred lake, Lhamo Lhatso. In this small lake surrounded by tall mountains, Tibetans believed they could see fleeting images of the future. The weather

THE DALAI LAMA AND REINCARNATION

Tibetan Buddhists believe in reincarnation: that when a person dies he or she is born again and again into a series of different lives until nirvana—a state of ultimate peace— is reached. It takes many lifetimes of struggling through hardships, prayer, and meditation to achieve nirvana. Every good deed you do brings you closer to nirvana, and every bad deed pushes you farther away.

The Living Buddhas are saints who have come so far along the path to nirvana that they could end their cycle of death and rebirth, but instead they choose to keep being reborn to help the rest of humanity. Tibetans believe that the Dalai Lama is one of these special beings; he has chosen to come back to this life many times to guide and protect the people of Tibet. The first Dalai Lama was born in 1391. Every time a Dalai Lama dies, his successor must be found through visions, dreams, omens, and tests.

changes quickly there, from rain, snow, or hail to clear skies, and the changes are reflected in the waters of the lake.

First the regent saw the Tibetan letters *Ah, Ka* and *Ma* form in the lake's depths. Next he saw a monastery with three stories and a gold and turquoise roof. A white road led to a house with a brown and white dog sitting outside. Later the regent dreamed of this same house. It had a very peculiar twisted eavestrough, and a little boy was standing in the courtyard. The regent concluded that the letter *Ah* stood for Amdo, a province in northeastern Tibet. *Ka* referred to the monastery at Kumbum, which had three stories and a beautiful gold and turquoise roof. *Ma* pointed to a smaller monastery nearby.

A group of high officials and monks set off for Amdo to find the house with the strange eavestrough. After many months of searching they found it in a little village called Takster. The house's gutters were made of juniper branches that had been carved out to allow the rain to flow through them. The monks went to the house in disguise so they could look for the new spiritual leader without anyone knowing who they were. A brown and white dog barked at them when they came to the door. Inside they found Lhamo, who loved visitors. Putting all the signs together, along with the results of the tests and the obvious intelligence and confidence of the little boy, the monks had no doubts: they had found their new Dalai Lama.

Hidden in the heart of Asia, between India and China, Tibet lies on a high plateau with towering mountain ranges and wide, lonely plains. The mountains are so high and the air is so thin that only certain types of animals can live there, such as the huge, hairy, and extremely useful yak. Because Tibet is so difficult to get to, the ancient culture that developed in the Land of the Snows survived almost without changing into the middle of the twentieth century. Tibetans did their best to keep themselves isolated from strangers and outside influences so that they could preserve their religion and their way of life.

At the time of the Dalai Lama's birth in 1935, Tibetan people lived much the way they had in medieval times, without modern conveniences like electricity, cars, telephones, or flush toilets. Tibet was the only place in the world where monks ran the government. The Buddhist religion influenced every aspect of life. People went on pilgrimages to holy places, and they prayed with prayer beads (rosaries) and prayer wheels (cylinders with written

Tibet 1959

Prayer wheels are cylinders filled with scrolls of paper. As they spin, people read the prayers written on the scrolls.

prayers inside them). Elaborate ceremonies and parades marked holidays, and prayer flags fluttered on the roofs of houses and tents and along roadsides and bridges. Tibetans even flew kites inscribed with prayers, knowing that the words would be closer to God in the sky.

At that time there were about 6,000 monasteries in Tibet. Nearly every community of any size had its own. Some monasteries were small and simple, with only a handful of monks. Others were like small castles, where many monks lived and studied. Monasteries had been the source of education, culture, and religion in Tibet for hundreds of years. Many families sent at least one young boy to a monastery to be trained as a monk. The greatest monastery was at Lhasa, known as the Forbidden City, because for many centuries no foreigners were allowed to go there. The Dalai Lamas ruled for hundreds of years in this ancient, hidden capital.

A monk carries the four-year-old Dalai Lama on the way to
Lhasa to take his place on the Lion Throne as the king and
spiritual ruler of Tibet.

When Lhamo was four years old, the monks decided he was
old enough to make the long journey from Amdo to Lhasa, where
he would be formally installed as the fourteenth Dalai Lama. It
was a long, difficult journey by caravan over poor roads that
crossed rivers, mountains, and wide, lonely plains. Lhamo rode
inside a special royal palanquin with yellow curtains accompanied by his brother Lobsang, who was eight. Every so often the

drivers leading the mules had to stop when fights broke out between the two boys inside the litter. Then their mother would be summoned to put her foot down. She would open the curtains and as likely as not find Lhamo grinning smugly and Lobsang crying. Although Lhamo was much smaller, he usually had the upper hand because Lobsang was too kind-hearted to beat up his annoying little brother. Like most little boys, Lhamo took great pleasure in tormenting his sibling.

After three months, the caravan finally reached Lhasa in the fall of 1939, to be greeted by thousands of joyful Tibetans welcoming their new Dalai Lama to the city. The little boy was captivated by his warm reception and the outpouring of love from his people. He felt he was coming home.

Lhamo's entry into Lhasa marked the beginning of both his official life as the Dalai Lama and his training to be a Buddhist monk. When he was four and a half, his head was shaved and he took his novice vows (the promises a monk makes). Then he was dressed in the traditional maroon and yellow monk's robes he would wear for the rest of his life. In a sacred ceremony, he took his place on the Lion Throne in the great Potala Palace as the fourteenth Dalai Lama, the Living Buddha.

The Potala Palace loomed high on a hill above the city of Lhasa. The huge medieval fortress held an entire monastery, with chapels and a school for 175 monks, as well as government offices, libraries, storerooms, and treasure chambers. Within its four-meter (13-foot) thick walls were more than 1,000 rooms, 10,000 altars and 200,000 statues, as well as the tombs of several previous Dalai Lamas.

The Dalai Lama lived on the top floor, in the same bedroom where previous Dalai Lamas had slept since the castle was built in 1696. Ancient curtains hung on the walls, ancient dust lay

The Potala Palace, built in 1696, rises high above the city of Lhasa. The Dalai Lama lived in this huge, freezing palace from the age of four until he fled Tibet when he was twenty-three.

behind them, and an altar held yak-butter lamps and offerings of water and food for the Buddha. A troop of mice came and nibbled at these offerings every day, then ran up and down the curtains of the bed at night. The young Dalai Lama lay among his cushions, listening to the drip, drip of their pee. He said later that he liked the mice—they were so small and beautiful, and they were company for him. But the Dalai Lama was not totally without human playmates; he had his brother Lobsang with him until he was eight. He also made friends with the sweepers who kept the floors clean and polished, and he roped them into playing endless games of toy soldiers with him.

The Potala Palace was dark and cold, with long, shadowy corridors. The Dalai Lama much preferred his summer residence, Norbulingka. Two miles outside Lhasa, it was a group of buildings set within a walled park. Peacocks, parrots, geese, and cranes roamed freely through the gardens, along with the Dalai Lama's dogs—Tibetan mastiffs and a Pekinese. His private zoo at Norbulingka housed the exotic animals he had been given as gifts: camels, leopards, a tiger, and an elephant. His parents had a house within the grounds, and the Dalai Lama could visit them every day. While he was still small he liked to sneak over to their place and eat pork or eggs—two foods forbidden to monks. Once, when one of his attendants scolded him for doing this, the little boy shouted at him to go away.

DON'T KILL THAT FLY!

In the Tibetan form of Buddhism, all life is sacred. It is wrong to kill even an ant or a fly. When digging new roads or foundations for buildings, the workers may hold up the job up for hours while they patiently save the life of each worm their shovels uncover.

Despite their respect for all life, Tibetans aren't usually vegetarian. It would be very hard to survive in their harsh environment without eating meat. If someone else kills the animal, a Tibetan Buddhist can eat it.

The Dalai Lama used to watch huge herds of yaks being taken to the slaughterhouse every fall. He felt so sorry for them that he sent his servants out to buy as many as they could and save them from the butcher's knife. He may have saved the lives of as many as 10,000 yaks over the years.

THE MIGHTY YAK

Kids in Tibet often treat the yak as if it were a family pet. These strange creatures live longer than cats or dogs: between 20 and 25 years. Tibetans would have a hard time surviving the harsh climate of their country with the help of the versatile yak.

The yak has provided Tibetans with food, shelter, and clothing for centuries. Closely related to the cow, the yak stands between 1.2 and 1.8 meters (4 and 6 feet) tall. It has a very long, thick coat and weighs more than 450 kilograms (1,000 pounds).

The yak can carry goods and people over rough terrain, and it doesn't mind the frigid Tibetan winters. Its skin and fur are used to make clothes, tents, ropes, and even boats. Its meat can be eaten, but its milk is especially prized by Tibetans.

Yak milk is made into yak butter, one of the staples of the Tibetan diet. It has a particularly sour taste that Tibetans love. Like everything else about the yak, the butter is extremely versatile. Tibetans add it to their tea, burn it in lamps, and use it to protect their skin from frost-bite. Even yak dung doesn't go to waste: it is used as fuel for fires.

Gradually, though, the young Dalai Lama grew accustomed to his new life and the restrictions it brought. There was something in him, right from the beginning, that took to his role naturally. He had great dignity for a small child, and he learned to sit still for hours during religious ceremonies, although the longer ones were a torture when he had to go to the bathroom. He worried about controlling his bladder as much as about remembering the words of the difficult texts he had to recite. Except on formal occasions, the servants and monks who were around the Dalai Lama every day treated him like any other child, and perhaps this kept him from being spoiled.

The Dalai Lama's schoolroom was a cold verandah outside his bedroom. Every morning he woke up at six and spent one hour in prayer and meditation. Then he had breakfast, which was tea with yak butter and tsampa porridge with honey or caramel. Salty tea with lots of yak butter instead of milk is a favorite drink in Tibet. The warm butter fat keeps out the cold. Tsampa, a flour made from barley, is another staple food there. The hour or so after breakfast was given over to penmanship, which he had to study until he was 13. Tibetans have two different scripts, one for everyday writing and one for religious manuscripts, so learning to write was a complicated process that took a lot of practice.

Memorization came next: every day the Dalai Lama had to commit a piece of Buddhist scripture to memory. At 10 o'clock he would attend government meetings, where he learned as much as he could by listening to the officials. After lunch came the heavy subjects, which were divided into major and minor. The major ones included Buddhist philosophy, Sanskrit (an ancient Indian language), medicine, logic, and Tibetan art and culture. Some of the minor subjects he learned were drama, poetry, music, and astrology.

At four in the afternoon came tea, and after that debating with the monks. Debating is a form of arguing in public. In Tibet, debating was a bit like theater or dance, with special gestures and hand-clapping. People would gather in the courtyard of a monastery to watch the monks debate, usually about the meaning of a particular piece of religious writing, and the most admired debaters were those who had the sharpest wits and used humor against their opponents. The Dalai Lama began to study debating when he was 10, and by the time he was 14 he could hold his own in debate with the abbot (the monk in charge of a monastery).

WHIPS AND READING

When the Dalai Lama first started his lessons, he was taught to read with his brother, Lobsang, for company. Hanging on the schoolroom wall were two whips: one made of yellow silk and one of leather. Their teachers explained that the yellow whip was for the Dalai Lama and the leather whip for his brother, and the two little boys lived in fear of them. A teacher had only to glance over at the whips for boys to tremble and try a little harder.

The Dalai Lama said in later years that these whips were more for show than anything else. He was never whipped, but very occasionally the leather one was used on poor Lobsang, who wasn't quite as quick as his brother at learning his lessons.

All of the Dalai Lama's teachers said they were astounded by his quick intelligence and abilities as a student. But the Dalai Lama himself claims he was "a very reluctant pupil and disliked all subjects equally."

At 5:30 p.m. the Dalai Lama had some free time. One of his favorite things to do was to look at the outside world through his telescope from the palace roof. Since he was never allowed to be around ordinary people or to go down into the city except on formal occasions, this was a chance to see how people lived.

After supper the Dalai Lama went down to a courtyard to walk. He was supposed to recite scripture and pray as he exercised, but he often found his mind wandering off into daydreams. At nine o'clock he went to bed. The monks would often tell him scary bedtime stories, and then he was left alone in the darkness, with his imagination and the mice.

The senior monks, political advisors, and religious scholars who were responsible for the Dalai Lama's education had one goal in mind: grooming him to be the best possible spiritual leader and king of Tibet. His entire life was devoted to these goals. The traditions and rituals surrounding his position had remained unchanged for hundreds of years.

The Dalai Lama always had a group of servants with him if he left the palace. When he moved to the palace at Norbulingka every spring, hundreds of people joined in a procession that included musicians, soldiers, bodyguards, and monks, all in colorful costumes. The Dalai Lama was carried in the middle in a yellow palanquin. His songbirds were transported carefully in their cages, and his possessions were wrapped in yellow silk. The entire city came out to watch him pass. People were so moved to see the Living Buddha that some of them cried, and they all bowed their heads or prostrated themselves on the ground. This was the standard greeting for the Dalai Lama: anyone coming into his presence had to lie down on the ground in front of him.

As the Dalai Lama grew older, he sometimes longed for a more ordinary life, with less formality and ritual. When he heard boys playing outside he wished he could just have fun the way they did. And he was extremely curious about the world beyond Tibet.

When he was about 13, he made friends with Heinrich Harrer, an Austrian mountain climber. Harrer was one of the few outsiders who had managed to get into the Forbidden City of Lhasa, after many adventures and hardships along the way. He first came to the palace to help the Dalai Lama with the electricity for his movie projector, and soon he was coming several times a week to teach him whatever he could about the outside world. Harrer helped the Dalai Lama with his English, too, and taught him geography and arithmetic. The Dalai Lama had countless questions that Harrer did his best to answer, such as "How does an atomic bomb work?" and "How is a jet plane built?"

One of the great things about being the Dalai Lama was the presents: people from all over the world sent him wonderful gifts. He was always fascinated by how things worked, and he loved taking apart watches and clocks and then putting them back together again. He did this with a movie projector that had been a gift from the British royal family. He also took apart the

THE MANY NAMES OF THE DALAI LAMA

Sometimes you can tell how important people are by the number of names they have. The Dalai Lama's many names, official and unofficial, show how his people feel about him. Officials call him Gyalpo Rinpoche (Precious King), others call him Yeshe Norbu (Wish-fulfilling Gem), and his family and friends called him Kundun (The Presence). But now he is usually referred to simply as the Dalai Lama, which means "Ocean of Wisdom."

gold watch given to him by the Americans, and the mechanical cars, boats, trains, and airplanes sent to him by other foreign governments. His very favorite toy was Meccano, a popular metal construction set that came with real electrical engines, and by the time he was 15 he had collected all the different Meccano sets that were available.

The Dalai Lama's biggest playthings (aside from his elephant) were a couple of cars that someone had given to the thirteenth Dalai Lama. These were stored away because there were no paved roads in Tibet to drive them on. The Dalai Lama found a driver, though, and together they got one of the cars going. One day, the Dalai Lama couldn't resist taking it for a joyride around the garden, and he crashed into a tree. Like any other kid, he tried to hide what he'd done from the grownups, fixing the broken headlight as best he could.

Cold, dark, and gloomy it may have been, but the Potala Palace had at least one thing to recommend it: hidden treasure. Think of your own basement or storage cupboards and multiply their contents by hundreds of years of collecting things, many of them priceless gifts from foreign officials. The Dalai Lama and his brother Lobsang found heaps of silver and gold in the storerooms, but way more fun were the old swords, guns, and armor. One of the Dalai Lama's most fascinating finds was a set of illustrated books about the First World War, and he studied these for hours.

Despite the distractions, though, of toys, treasure, and all that Heinrich Harrer could teach him about the world beyond the mountains, the center of the Dalai Lama's world was his religion. As he studied to be a monk, he spent many hours in prayer and meditation. He took part in ceremonies and festivals throughout the year, and went on retreats where he prayed and meditated nearly all day for three weeks at a time.

Tibetans believe that their country is protected by Chenrezig, the god of compassion, and that the Dalai Lama is this god's human form. They came to the Dalai Lama to be blessed, and carried little pictures of him around with them to keep them safe. Everything the new Dalai Lama learned was to prepare him to take on this role as the god-king of Tibet when he turned 17.

But in 1950 the Chinese invaded Tibet, and everything changed. It started with an omen. One day in the summer of 1950, the country was rocked by several huge explosions, and a red glow appeared in the sky. Earth tremors shook the buildings and rattled the doors. It was probably a series of earthquakes, with the layers of rock shifting deep below the mountains' surface. But the Tibetans took the disturbance as a sign of trouble to come.

And trouble did come that October, in the shape of 80,000 Chinese troops who moved into eastern Tibet. The Chinese Communists had just won the revolution in China, and they wanted Tibet's territory for themselves. The Communists also believed that religion was poison and that it kept people backward and poor. So they set out to destroy Buddhism in Tibet, and to transform all Tibetans into good Communists.

The small Tibetan army of 8,500 men was no match for the Chinese war machine. The Tibetans had few weapons and were not well trained. They were slaughtered. Some escaped and went into hiding in the mountains. From there they continued to fight the Chinese, by carrying out raids whenever they could. The Chinese called their invasion "the peaceful liberation of Tibet," alleging that they were helping Tibet and bringing modern improvements to the country.

Many people in Tibet came to believe it was time for the Dalai Lama to take over the leadership of his country, even though he was only 15 and had not finished his preparations to become ruler. His country needed him. The Dalai Lama was scared, and he didn't feel ready, but he knew he had to do his best to help his people.

Wearing a green sash around his waist—a color chosen by the astrologers—the Dalai Lama was enthroned in a ceremony held at dawn in a dark chapel. The climax came when he was presented with the Golden Wheel. The tradition of the Golden Wheel comes from an ancient Indian custom, in which a wheel from the king's war chariot is used to represent his earthly power. In Tibetan Buddhism, it also represents the Buddha's teaching. As the spiritual leader of his people, as well as their king, the Dalai Lama was the Emperor of Peace, the turner of the Golden Wheel of truth. His childhood was over.

The End of the Story

The Dalai Lama, now Tibet's official leader, sent out messengers to Britain, the United States, and India to appeal for support against the Chinese invasion. But China was very powerful, and no one wanted to start a war with the well-armed country. The Dalai Lama tried to negotiate with China directly, too. The government made many promises about letting Tibetans follow their religion and govern themselves, but sooner or later they broke them all.

The Tibetan freedom fighters hiding in the hills kept up their raids, and other Tibetans gathered in cities and towns to demonstrate against the Chinese invaders. Finally, in 1959, when he was 23 years old, the Dalai Lama himself was threatened. It looked as if the Chinese would capture and most likely kill him. Although he did not want to leave his country, he realized that he could best help his people from outside Tibet. Disguising himself as an ordinary soldier, he managed to escape. Along with his family, his tutors, and some government officials, he walked for two weeks through the wild lands of Tibet to the Indian border, protected by a group of Tibetan soldiers. When they crossed the border, the refugees were greeted by a crowd of journalists and hundreds of telegrams, letters, and messages from well-wishers all over the world.

The Dalai Lama continues to lead his people from exile. Here he sits on his throne in the simple robes of a monk.

Today the Dalai Lama is an inspiration to people all over the world.

The Dalai Lama has never gone back to Tibet. About 120,000 Tibetans have since joined him in Dharamsala, India, where they have been given a safe place to rebuild their lives and to preserve their religion and culture. The Chinese have continued to try to stamp out all religious practices in Tibet, destroying nearly all 6,000 monasteries. Through famine, war, and persecution, over one million Tibetans have died as a result of the Chinese invasion.

Tibetans believe that the Dalai Lama represents the spirit of compassion in human form. Compassion means caring about other people, especially when they are in trouble, and his job has been to care for his people through the worst crisis of their history. The Dalai Lama has established a Tibetan government in exile, and he has brought in many reforms to make the government democratic. He has spread his particular form of love and caring throughout the world, and he has thousands of supporters who are not Tibetans, but who believe in his message of peace and non-violence. He is appreciated for his sense of humor and his patience, as well as for his deep spiritual beliefs. The Dalai Lama travels all over the world, inspiring people by his example. People love to hear him laugh, which he does often. In 1989 he was awarded the Nobel Prize for Peace.

When little Lhamo Dhondrub was chosen to be the fourteenth Dalai Lama, it was clear that he had a great destiny. The twists and turns of fate have led him far from the hidden Land of Snows, into a much larger world where he has had a profound impact.

This is a prayer that he says inspires him and gives him the determination to continue:

For as long as space endures,
And for as long as living beings remain,
Until then may I, too, abide
To dispel the misery of the world.

Afterword

The days of the semi-divine, all-powerful kings and queens are over. Although there are still kings and queens in the world, very few truly rule their countries. Their role has been reduced to symbolic leadership of their people. Many lead lives of wealth and privilege, but they no longer hold the absolute power they once enjoyed.

Despite its reduced importance, royalty survives. Perhaps the royals' popularity comes from their link with the past or from their glamorous lives. Or perhaps it comes from something deeper. People still cling to the notion of the divine right of kings—that royal blood carries a mysterious power.

There is one child ruler in the world today whose future life will be shaped by the circumstances of his birth. King Oyo Nyimba Kabamba Iguru Rukidi IV of the Toro Kingdom in Uganda, Africa, is a teenager who spends half his life as a normal boy and the other half as the revered traditional king of one million subjects. Although he has no political power, his position has great spiritual meaning for his people.

In 1992 , when Oyo was a three, he inherited the title of king from his father, who died suddenly of a heart attack. He has grown up with his mother and sister in a house in the suburbs of Kampala, the capital of Uganda. He goes to a private school, he loves playing soccer and listening to African rock music, and he has a couple of dogs and a cat as pets. But, on ceremonial occasions, Oyo travels the four hours to his palace in Toro, dons the traditional robes of a king, and presides over rituals sacred to the citizens of Toro.

As Oyo grows up, he will take on more of his role as the cultural leader of his people, representing their interests in the outside world and inspiring them as a symbol of both their past and their future. His life will never be completely his own, as his duty to his country and his people will always shape his decisions and his destiny. Just like the many child monarchs in the past, he has had to grow up fast. Although being a king in modern Africa is far different from what it was when Tutankhamun took the pharaoh's throne 3,000 years ago, Oyo and Tut have both had to somehow fulfill the great expectations of the people around them, and be kids—who rule.

Sources and Further Reading

THE IMMORTAL PHARAOH: TUTANKHAMUN OF EGYPT

Ardagh, Philip. *The Secret Diary of Prince Tutankhamun*. Franklin Watts. London: 1998.

Hawass, Zahi. *Tutankhamun: The Mystery of the Boy King*. National Geographic. Washington: 2005.

Houlihan, Patrick F. "Tutankhamun's Wardrobe." *Ancient Egypt*. Vol 4, Issue 1 July/August 2003, p. 46.

Macdonald, Fiona. *The World in the Time of Tutankhamen*. Chelsea House. Philadelphia: 2001.

Tames, Richard. *Ancient Egyptian Children*. Heinemann Library. Chicago: 2003.

Treasures of Tutankhamun. Metropolitan Museum of Art. New York: 1976.

QUEEN ON THE RUN: MARY QUEEN OF SCOTS

Guy, John. *"My Heart is My Own": The Life of Mary Queen of Scots*. Fourth Estate. HarperCollins. London: 2004.

Lasky, Kathryn. *Mary, Queen of Scots: Queen without a Country*. The Royal Diaries Series. Scholastic: New York, 2002.

Steel, David, and Judy. *Mary Stuart's Scotland: The Landscapes, Life and Legends of Mary Queen of Scots*. George Weidenfeld and Nicolson. London: 1987.

THE GIRL BORN TO BE KING: QUEEN CHRISTINA OF SWEDEN

Buckley, Veronica. *Christina, Queen of Sweden: The Restless Life of a European Eccentric*. Fourth Estate. HarperCollins. New York: 2004.

Lewis, Paul. *Queen of Caprice: A Biography of Kristina of Sweden*. Holt, Rinehart and Winston. New York: 1962.

Masson, Georgina. *Queen Christina*. Martin Secker & Warburg. London: 1968.

Meyer, Caroline. *Kristina: The Girl King*. The Royal Diaries Series. Scholastic. New York: 2003.

THE MAKE-BELIEVE EMPEROR: EMPEROR PUYI OF CHINA

Behr, Edward. *The Last Emperor.* Macdonald & Co. Ltd. London: 1987.
"I had no freedom ..." quote from page 132.

Dorn, Frank. *The Forbidden City: The Biography of a Palace.* Charles
Scribner's Sons. New York: 1970.

Pu Yi, Henry. *The Last Manchu. The Autobiography of Henry Pu Yi.*
Edited by Paul Kramer. Weidenfeld and Nicolson. London:
1967. "Fire in his heart ..." quote from page 49.

BORN (AGAIN) TO RULE (AGAIN): THE DALAI LAMA OF TIBET

Avedon, John F. *In Exile from the Land of Snows.* Random House. New
York: 1986.

Bruycker, Daniel de, and Martine Noblet. *Tibet.* Barron's Educational
Series, Inc. New York: 1995.

Gyatso, Tenzin. *Freedom in Exile: The Autobiography of the Dalai Lama.*
HarperCollins. New York: 1990. "A very reluctant pupil ..."
quote from page 25. "For as long as space endures ..." quote
from page 271.

Harrer, Heinrich. *Seven Years in Tibet.* HarperCollins. London: 1997.

Samphel, Thubten and Tendar. *The Dalai Lamas of Tibet.* Roli Books
Pvt. Ltd. New Delhi: 2000.

Photo Credits

25, cover main, AP/Wide World Photo/Egypt's Supreme Council of Antiquities/HO; **93,** AP/Wide World Photo; **110,** AP/Wide World Photo/Ashwini Bhatia; **111,** AP/Wide World Photo/Roberto Candia

10, The Art Archive/Egyptian Museum, Cairo/Dagli Orti; **16,** The Art Archive/British Museum/Jacqueline Hyde; **19,** 1332-1322 BC: discovered by Howard Carter in 1922. Credit: The Art Archive/Egyptian Museum, Cairo/Dagli Orti (A); **55, back cover right,** painting by Pelagio Palagi. Credit: The Art Archive/Galleria d'Arte Moderna, Milan/Dagli Orti (A); **62,** painting by Jacob Heinrich Elbfas. Credit: The Art Archive/Gripsholm Castle, Sweden/Dagli Orti (A); **65,** painting by Sebastien Bourdon. Credit: The Art Archive/Museo del Prado, Madrid

15, Copyright: Griffith Institute, Oxford

23, © iStockphoto Inc./Vladimir Pomortsev; **31,** © iStockphoto Inc./Joshi Fullop; **41,** © iStockphoto Inc./Bart Parren; **74,** © iStockphoto Inc./Chee Khiang Sng; **75, cover left first,** © iStockphoto Inc./Andrew Berndt; **78,** © iStockphoto Inc./Josie Drever Chu; **81,** © iStockphoto Inc./Leon Zhu; **97,** © iStockphoto Inc./Jason Maehl; **100,** © iStockphoto Inc./Springboard, Inc.; **102,** © iStockphoto Inc./Vera Bogaerts; **endpapers,** © iStockphoto Inc./Heidi Kristensen

33, cover right first and second, LC-USZC4-10768; **50,** reproduction of painting by Julius Schrader, 187-. c1903. LC-USZ62-47596; **71 left, back cover left,** 1909. LC-USZ62-97149; **71 right, cover left second,** LC-DIG-ggbain-06343; **83,** LC-DIG-ggbain-21677; **86,** LC-DIG-ggbain-21678. All courtesy Library of Congress, Prints & Photographs Division

39, Bibliothèque nationale de France

45, *Book of Hours.* France, s. XV. 1v and 1r. Courtesy Beinecke Rare Book and Manuscript Library, Yale University

56, painting by Govert Camphuysen, 1661. Credit: Stockholm City Museum/Stockholms Stadsmuseum

60, engraving, 1633. © Bibliothèque des Arts decoratifs, Paris, France/Archives Charmet/The Bridgeman Art Library

98, © Bettmann/CORBIS

Acknowledgements

As always with a book, it took many hands to make it happen. A big thank-you to everyone at Annick Press who helped bring it to life. You are a great team and fun to work with! Barbara Pulling's thoughtful editing was much appreciated. My daughter Zoe helped me come up with the original idea and she was always enthusiastic, no matter how many times I asked her to "just read this chapter again." My friend Anita Levin guided me through the dark patches with her unique blend of wisdom and humor. And finally, my heartfelt gratitude to Evelyn and Graham Cotter, my dear parents, who keep me going.

—Charis Cotter

Index

Index

Index